QRL POETRY SERIES:

VOLUME XX: E. G. BURROWS' verse play based on the diaries of Fanny Kemble, actress, abolitionist, feminist; important first poetry books by BRIAN SWANN and REGINALD GIBBONS; the debut appearance of M. SLOTNICK; and DAVID GALLER's third book. $15 p.

VOLUME XXI: JANE FLANDER's, JEANNE FOSTER HILL's, and JOHN MORGAN's mature first books; a translation of Canadian poet ANNE HEBERT by POULIN; a play by SIDNEY SULKIN. $15 p.

VOLUME XXII: debuts by MAIRI MACINNES; DAVID BARTON, "possibly this year's most distinguished"—*Hudson Review*; PHYLLIS THOMPSON's third book; Brazilian poet CARLOS NEJAR translated by PICCIOTO; and Korean poet, SO CHONGJU, by McCANN $10 p.

VOLUME XXIII: JANE HIRSHFIELD's lyrical first book; MARGUERITE GUZMAN BOUVARD's journey between Trieste and America; CHRISTOPHER BURSK's "exhilarating" second book; one of Poland's most splendid poets, WISLAWA SZYMBORSKA, translated by S. OLDS, DREBIK, and FLINT; and Swedish poet LARS GUSTAFSSON, translated by Gustafsson with Australian poet PHILIP MARTIN. $15 p.

VOLUME XXIV: celebrates the poignant poetry of "one of America's best poets"—(Ashbery), *DAVID SCHUBERT: Works and Days.* All of Schubert's mature poems are presented; in addition, a biography, composed of his early poems and letters, intertwined with other's memoirs and letters, dramatically recreates this poet of and in the '40s. "A remarkable document: haunting, suspenseful, original, deeply moving" (Oates). Essays on Schubert by Ashbery, Ehrenpreis, Ignatow, Wright. $10 p.

VOLUME XXV: features REUEL DENNEY's poem on architecture; translations by SWANN and SCHEER of Spaniard RAFAEL ALBERTI; first books by NANCY ESPOSITO and LARRY KRAMER; and a poetic foray into a den of deconstructionists by ANNE CARSON. $20 cloth only.

VOLUME XXVI: JAMES BERTOLINO's third volume; beginnings and endings by novelist WARREN CARRIER; FREDERICK FEIRSTEIN's explorations into his rowdy origins; vivid first books by JULIA MISHKIN and JOSEPH POWELL; and SHURBANOV's and KESSLER's translation of Bulgarian poet NICOLAI KANTCHEV. $20 cloth only.

VOLUME XXVII: the distinguished Welsh poet and doctor DANNIE ABSE'; the premier Portuguese poet EUGENIO DE ANDRADE translated by LEVITIN; JOAN ALESHIRE's second book; DAVID KELLER's poised and skillful first book; and PETER STAMBLER's dramatic historical sequence on the Schumann family. $20 cloth only.

VOLUME XXVIII-XXIX: QRL's 45th anniversary prizewinners: REG SANER, JEANNE McGAHEY (one of *Voice Literary Supplement's* "Best" books of the year;) JAROLD RAMSEY and CRAIG POWELL. $15 p.

Institutional and cloth price :$20

Quarterly
Review of

EDITED BY T. & R. WEISS

Literature

POETRY SERIES X
VOLUME XXX

JEAN NORDHAUS
My Life in Hiding

BRUCE BOND
The Anteroom of Paradise

GERALDINE C. LITTLE
Women: In the Mask and Beyond

B.H. FAIRCHILD
Local Knowledge

JUDITH KROLL
Our Elephant & That Child

26 HASLET AVENUE, PRINCETON, NEW JERSEY 08540

ACKNOWLEDGEMENTS: Some of the poems in this volume were first published in these magazines or books:

JEAN NORDHAUS: *American Poetry Review, Ascent, The Gettysburg Review, The Hollins Critic, Kansas Quarterly, New Virginia Review, Passages North, Phoebe, TheWashington Review, and West Branch.*

BRUCE BOND: *The Antioch Review, Apalachee Quarterly, The Chariton Review, The Denver Quarterly, The Georgia Review, Kansas Quarterly, The Missouri Review, Negative Capability, The New Republic, The Journal, Pacific Review, Ploughshares, Poet and Critic, Poetry, Poetry Northwest, Prarie Schooner, The Quarterly, Salmagundi, Shenandoah, Sonora Review, Southwest Review, Stone Country, West Branch.* Several poems appeared in *The Ivory Hours,* a chapbook (Heatherstone Press).

GERALDINE C. LITTLE: *Nimrod* (Neruda Prize, 1989); *Raccoon; Women's Studies Quarterly; Massachusetts Review; Japanophile; Seneca Review; Stone Country;* the anthologies *Bluestones and Salt Hay* and *Only Morning in Her Shoes; Shenandoah; Minnesota Review; New Jersey Poetry Journal; Columbia; The Denny Prize Poems Anthology; The Literary Review; The Journal of N.J. Poets; Poet Lore; The Croton Review; Blue Unicorn; U.S. #1 Worksheets.* "For Jacqueline du Pré" won the Cecil Hemley Award, (Poetry Society of America) "In the House of Special Purpose" won an Associated Writing Programs Anniversary Award)

B.H. FAIRCHILD: *The American Writer,AWP Newsletter, Black Warrior Review Cincinnati Review, Colorado Review, Georgia Review, Hudson Review, Jacaranda Review, Oxford Magazine, Poetry, Prairie Schooner, Salmagundi, Southern Poetry Review, Southern Review, TriQuarterly.* Several poems appeared in the chapbook "The System of Which the Body Is One Part" (State Street Press and "Flight,"(Devil's Millhopper Press.) The author is grateful for support from the National Endowment for the Atrts.

J
UDITH KROLL: *The Antioch Review; Connecticut Poetry Revie, The Iowa Review, New Letters, The New Yorker:* "At Seven Thousand Feet," "Loving Someone Else," *The North American Review, Poetry, Poetry Now, Revista de Occidente, Sierra Madre Review, The Southern Review,Tendril.* The author wishes also to thank the National Endowment for the Arts for their assistance.

Assistants: Victor Fanucchi, Helen Yantchisin, John LaPlante,
Anne-Lise Francais

for RRN, my love

JEAN NORDHAUS

My Life in Hiding

JEAN NORDHAUS was born in Baltimore, Maryland. She received her BA from Barnard College in philosophy and a doctorate in German Literature from Yale University. She is the author of two prior volumes of poetry: a chapbook, *A Language of Hands*, published by SCOP in 1982; and *A Bracelet of Lies*, which was published by Washington Writers' Publishing House in 1987. From 1980 to 1983, she ran the poetry programs at the Folger Shakespeare Library and (in 1982-83) the PEN/Faulkner Award for Fiction. She was Meralmikjan Fellow in Poetry at Breadloaf in 1987.

CONTENTS

NOTES FROM THE CAVE
Under the Sign of Isadora   8
Kindertotenlieder   8
Twenty-two Windows   10
My Bolshevik Years   11
Notes from the Cave   12
Exploratory Surgery   13

ALPHABET GAMES
Discovering   16
Alphabet Games   17
The Sad Man   18
Norfolk   19
A Widow Reads *Robinson Crusoe*   21
The Cat   22
Deathwatch   23
Richard Casting a Melon   25

AN ACT OF TRANSLATION
The Black Scarf   27
Eating Crow   28
Like Wild Geese   29
The Page Turner   30
Womb Riddles   31
Other Voices   33
"Space Alien Newspaper Found at UFO Site"   34
Weather Channel   35
Commerce   36
Caballos   37
Miracles   38

QUARTET WITH PROGRAM NOTES BY COMPOSER
Quartet with Program Notes   41

MY LIFE IN HIDING

How We Speak to One Another with Dreams 48
Curtain Call 49
Willingly 50
New York Landscape, 1908 51
Opening Oysters 52
Woman Hasn't Slept a Wink in Thirty Years 53
Housekeeping in Heaven 54
The Fires 55
The Pond 56
Traveler 57
The Dream of Packing 58
My Life in Hiding 60

AFTERWORD 61

NOTES
FROM THE CAVE

UNDER THE SIGN OF ISADORA,

my lonely mother taught me dancing.
It was afternoon, her cleaning done.
We climbed to the carpeted room
under the roof. Sunlight had entered
before us, warm prayer rugs unrolled
on the carpet. We took off our shoes
and closed the door.

Whatever she did, I repeated.
When she raised her arms
to touch the sky, I lifted mine.
If she bent low, sweeping the grass
with her arms, I did the same.
I would be water. In me
she would watch herself move between past

and future, my infant steps
continuing the figures hers began.
Now the waves commenced whose origins
pulsed before music, a rocking
like the motion of a wing, the gesture
swelling, flowing through her body
into mine, out through my fingertips
into the world.

KINDERTOTENLIEDER

Someone is dying.
Turn the volume high, so we can hear
above these shrieks, the green
meadow far beyond. Who is walking there?
A father, a child in an organdy dress.

He grabs her gently under the arms
and lifts her onto the altar, a stone slab
nested in flowers, touched by light winds.

Why were we so caught up, my father and I,
in those songs about the death of children?
Rocked on swells of sound,
we lay on the living room rug after dinner
letting Kathleen Ferrier's bosomy

contralto smother us in folds of velvet.
My mother is in the kitchen, holding her ears.
She does not want to know
about the dark thing between us—
the grief of Agamemnon

as he lowered the axe,
or how the blood embraced the blade.
She lowers the spoons into their caskets,
wraps the knives in their shrouds,
delivers the bright spears into darkness.

Why are we sad? I want to ask, What child
are we grieving for? My throat
is uncut and the rivers inside me
flow in both directions, leaving,
returning—Childhood,

I thought we were done
with one another, that you'd handed up
your last shards and nothing further
would come rising toward me
out of those drowned regions.

TWENTY-TWO WINDOWS

A woman the shape of a mushroom,
no bigger than a nine-year-old
and dressed in black
like one of those starlings
brought from abroad and set loose

on these shores, my grandmother
in our new house walked from room to room
on bandaged feet, turned and said
to my mother, voice rising to that grief-
soprano she saved for all deaths

and arrivals:
Twenty-two windows!
Imagine.

From the round, utterly
lightless womb, the warm hovel
in Mir, the long birth-tunnel
of steerage: Twenty-two breaches
for light, each day

a million crossings. Perhaps she remembered
her rooms in the city, the cavernous courtyard
far below with its trickle of watery light
and children who swam in that gloom
on legs pale as roots. Leaning

out of her life into ours like a plant
toward the sun, she said it again
with conviction—
as if she were taking an oath,
calling all her dead to witness.

MY BOLSHEVIK YEARS

In my youth
I mimed obeisance
to a haggard queen,
carried each day
the compost for her gardens.
At night I raged
and glittered
among the radicals.
I stormed the pantry,
circled the dining-
room, sailed manifestos
over the bannister
into the hallway.
I grew in myself
the seeds of force
my governors denied,
rehearsed for years
the excision of traitors,
rose at length
to power
in this government
of days to live
among the hours,
my house in flames.

NOTES FROM THE CAVE

I

Crouched at the top,
I can see only the bottoms of things
cut in half by a turn of the stair—
a rank of olive carpet treads,
half a doorway and the skirts
of chairs, my mother's shoes and ankles
as she passes devilled eggs, the crystal
chandelier dispensing trapezoids
of amethyst and amber light.

I hear my parents and their friends
conversing in a strange, new tongue, voices
rising to a fierce crescendo.
Bernie Goldbloom barks like a seal.
A low growl blossoms into gibbon-shrieks.
They are telling dirty jokes.

I am clean, maidenly
in my flannel gown, avid
to know. My perfect feet
encased in slippers. Soft down
covering my arms and legs.
Wolf Ears, they will call me
when they find me here. My father
has black hair all over his body.
I love him hopelessly, without reason
or measure. Sometimes when my mother passes close,
I catch the pungent scent of bear.

II

Now I take my turn in the lit room
at the oval table, reciting
my name. I have breasts.
I break bread with my hands.
I pass the platter of chicken or lamb.
At the punch-line, I laugh
with the others.   What little
I know, I know

indirectly. Outside are shadows
and sirens. Cars and searchbeams
cast the only light. Eyes wild
with fear, the stunned doe
sinks to her knees, offers a throat
to the rain.

EXPLORATORY SURGERY

Odd to think of hands inside my body.
Fingers like tourists
exploring the caves, light
striking rooms that have always been dark
—and what strange creatures painted
on the walls — running bison — the delicate
lace antlers, heavy haunches, arrows
launched from sinews of their kind.

My surgeon-shaman with his bone
dice, his mystic needles
has probing knives, ambiguous shears
and I who woke as a subject,

a mind full of schemes and reversals
lie docile now, a hat
turned inside out,
the scarf of blood pulled free.

I close my eyes, escape
to some fortunate island.
Soft wind blows all day. The sun
is huge and glitters like a surgeon's lamp.
The sea revolves in greenglass tiles.
And how to leave this place again. With
innocence? With luck? A small, white rabbit
pulled from the breast—benign.

Every setting out implies return.
But think of Scott, alone on his pole.
And of those hunter/artists
painting with such perishable skill
on walls from which air must be banished.

Yet now I rise to the sight
of my own blood
bright on the dressings
as visitors retreat from caverns
dimly understanding what they've seen.

ALPHABET GAMES

DISCOVERING

I'd like to say something profound
about this morning's executions, the getting
and spending, the dangerous swirl
of radiation that surrounds us, entering
the cell to interrupt the delicate
transcription of the genes

*

Death is no joke, no abstraction,
not even a measure we hold up
against our lives, the better
to see you with, my dear...

*

Last night I held a mirror to a mirror
and saw my naked back for the first time,
looming and close— like landing
in a place I never knew existed,
an alien geography of rills and hollows,
secret as the dark side of the moon.

*

Outside birds converse, carping
in their uninflected language, simple
argument of self, a singular
complaint.

*

On an island, a woman,
perhaps my mother.
She raises an arm to wave
because I am leaving, making the predicted
journey over water,
leaving the islands
where the woman is not standing.

ALPHABET GAMES

Before the waves broke into language
we lived as syllables
in a random sea. The bald sea-captain
and the nurse were waiting
to ferry us over. We stepped ashore
forgetting our passage, the circumstances
of our birth.

The trees in this land were silent.
Animals stood docile
under the yoke of their names:
> the Auk the Bear the Chamois the Falcon
> the Grebe the Rabbit the Rat the Spaniel
> wagging its tail.

Some girls in front of a tenement
were singing a jump-rope song.
One of these girls was my mother—quick-
handed, clever at jacks, nimblest
of all her sisters—as she jumped
she told her future,
spelling the name of her husband
and each of her children the street she would
live on the color the flavor her favorite
movie stars—All of it

came to be. I was born out of her mouth
as she jumped—a verb of action—
and I've been traveling uncertain ever since
while all around the sea churned and the bald
sea-captain came with the nurse—she began
reciting the seasons backward, recalling
all she had once uttered jumping
into being: the man the house the dog the child
the alphabet even the luminous

movie stars began to pale, her tongue the tongue
of a bell tolling losses—the promise the olive
the dove the ark the last word spoken—
her own engraved on stone as she vanished
into the surf of names.

THE SAD MAN

The first time, I saw him
standing on ship's deck
below the stacks. He took me
in his arms, I writhed away.
"We are like twin columns of black smoke,"
I said, "rising separately."

Next I found him
wandering the wild streets, his mind
rent with schisms and dreams.
I made a plan to rescue us,
so we could live in the world with others.
He laughed and called me by my secret name.

Once he came in green
and spoke with such beautiful pain
I tied my body to the headboard
not to follow him. The children
slept around me in their separate skins,
small breaths rising like moons, night trees
at the window crowding closer. This morning

he is at my door again, his tweed coat
garnished with twigs and stems, belted with rope.

I want to follow him through winding alleys
to a room with a narrow bed, to lie
on unwashed linens drinking bitter wine
until our mouths are red and sore.

But I shut the door.
I shut the door on the man who waits,
an unasked question, deep as my father
lying alone. I raise the blinds
and light breaks through, a white
fist on the rug, a fetal rose—
shape that lingers like a thought
or blessing— I love only laundry,
how it flees

and stays, tenacious,
swelling on the line
like ghosts of the living.

NORFOLK

"Every once in a while you look out there
and you see something disappearing," my father
said, speaking out of silence
in those days when he himself

was vanishing, his mind a ruined house
with crumbling cornices—
a shadow slipping
down the hall, a door
shutting just as you enter.

Of course, things kept appearing, too:
horses in the kitchen, riotous fiestas
under beds, doors opening
and slamming closed with small
explosions, manic winds and lachrymose
doldrums, a fine sift of dust
in the air.

Some days a window, flying open,
would release an old tableau
relived in rich detail:
the cracked guitar my brother bought
in Florence, every feather
of chagrin intact; songs or scents
of his Virginia childhood—rainbow
rings of gasoline on concrete
spreading stain, some bawdy homage to
           "...the girls from Norfolk.
           We don't smoke. We don't drink.
           Nor-fuck. Nor-fuck."

But mostly in my father's house
the lights are failing, corridors
rotting away, doors open
to a stairless precipice. In sealed-off

rooms, old servants lie, hands
folded over genitals, heads
oddly angled—as if they labored
at sleep, or were listening hard
for a word not yet spoken, a messenger
not yet arrived.

A WIDOW READS *ROBINSON CRUSOE*

Islanded, he must have been surprised
as she to find herself alone
in a season when even the winged
seeds of the maple come paired.

She admires his ingenuity
and how, bereft, he never lacks for comfort
how from the wreckage of hope, he framed
a habitation, fortified it
with a palisade of still-green sticks
that rooted in a self-renewing wall.

Slowly, taking pains, he taught himself
to fire cooking pots of clay, grind flour
for bread. Inventing agriculture,
rediscovering animal husbandry
and tailoring, he built a life
not so unlike the one he'd left
—but lonely. Once

from a felled tree, he carved a boat
so big he couldn't drag it to the water.
He started over, dug a smaller
vessel he could launch—for time
was all he had—twenty-eight
years, long enough to marry
and to raise a child....

It's night outside,
the telephone lies still.
Beside her looms the empty bed
unmapped and dangerous
as sleep. She pulls the afghan close
settles her glasses on her nose and reads.

THE CAT

The grey and white cat
splayed on a shoulder
of asphalt near a bridge sank
deeper, flattening into the roadbed
like someone settling in
to sleep or nuzzling closer
to a loved body. Patrolling
crows and buzzards never
troubled it. It just
grew smaller day by day
as my mother in her illness
had been growing smaller
until there was nothing
but a rug of dingy fur,
then a dark stain
on the pavement. Soon
even that was gone. Meanwhile
my mother's appetite improved.
She started gaining weight. And yet
whenever I drive across
that bridge, the ambushed
animal springs to mind, savage
as fear. Surely there is no road
between the cat's erasure and my mother's
brief reprieve. Only that love
prowling the winter lanes
for sustenance makes these wild leaps,
traveling back and forth between two cities.

DEATHWATCH

1

My mother is floating on her back
toward deeper water, every breath
an oarstroke propelling her on,
skin-folds like jonquils
dried in the vase, mere
tegument, all moisture gone.
In her face, the sheerest vestiges
of self: a web of tension
about shut eyes, slight worry-lines
along the brow. Soon even these
will be smoothed away. Nimble birds
skim past the window-screen, enmeshed
in nets of air.

2

The TV has been struck dumb,
its single eye gone milky-
blind. The body of light
shutting down to a sliver,
bird-cry caught in the lines.
At night the lamps keep vigil
like ancestral souls, their light
confined in haloes. This is how
the animal holds heat.

3

The last task is to reconcile myself to this,
loving even your husk, the ground
of transformation. Outside now, roses.
Death has planted itself in your bones
supplanting every feature. Your flesh
was the garden of darkness
from which my own life rose.
Surely I can teach myself to love
whatever still grows in that soil.

RICHARD CASTING A MELON

First, the melon itself, a huge brain,
interior network of nerve and vein
externalized. Then, Richard's hands,
blunt, square, capable, mixing the powder,
slapping and smoothing the paste as if gently
spanking a baby's butt, hurrying
before the plaster sets. Now we wait
while the great, lobed fruit in its bandages
heats and cools, as if that primitive mind
were giving birth to a new idea— the Genius
of Fire, or the Notion of the Soul. Next
Baptism, total immersion in water,
the mummy raised in its coffin,
a cautious tapping along the seams, our delicate
intake of breath as the shell falls open
in three segments and the melon
is lifted out, lovelier than ever,
leaving its own memorial behind, a hollow faithful
to this perfect, one-time-only melonness,
which can be filled and cast and filled
and so on down successive galleries
of absence and remembrance. Meanwhile the melon itself
is sliced and eaten. We do this
in the summer of our mother's death,
in the sweetness of flesh and the sharpness
of memory, here in the kitchen
where making begins.

AN ACT
OF TRANSLATION

THE BLACK SCARF

Every metaphor is an act of translation
says the poet at supper, turning
for another glass of wine
as smoke turns into a snake or bat
or grape to wine to blood.
It is dark in the theater
when he reads, his blackest, softest
cashmere silent in the wings.

Another word for death
glides out of his mouth
and disappears. A shudder
escapes the grey coat

draped across a velvet chair,
until what wound around his throat
coils in a pool on the floor
disguising itself as something lost.

EATING CROW

Blackbirds and crows if eaten as a matter of
necessity must be parblanched first.
"About Small Game Birds"
—The Joy of Cooking

There are many ways of cooking a blackbird
but all begin with a steep bath in the boiling vat.
Here sinew is softened, rancor removed.

Not until the fierce twins
Never and Always
slumber under the shield of sleep

and the raven will
flutters on cropped wings
can serious feasting begin—

Say, this large crow,
with its unlovely voice
and lively eye, or the grackle armored

in iridescence—
as simple
as swallowing words,

bolting a mouthful
of gristle and feathers
with something resembling grace.

LIKE WILD GEESE

pulled north on a thread of song
we make ourselves up as we go
following a line we cast ourselves, arrow
aimed at a life we imagine

inventing this house, the painted
furniture, closed garden,
flesh-colored walls,
dovecote and sigh of wind,
the blue-tailed lizard on the walk
stepping out of its skin
like a word out of silence

inventing the tree above the roof
the cream and yellow butterflies
brushing its leaves without hunger
and the woman who walks beneath
its branches, half-formed melody she hums,
the tree of language in her skull: seed,
stem, and leaf, the bird in the pond

and the bird in its branches, delicate
network of signs and stars
we steer along with awkward
vowels of longing—

THE PAGE TURNER

Accomplice
to the muse, I always sit
behind and to the left
of the pianist

with my ready hands,
eyes that see. But my heart
in its windowless room
can only count.

Requirements for this job
are to be short, love duty,
and desire a peaceful life

not to weep when streams flow gently
over the beautiful meadows to sea.
In furious battle
to preserve tranquility,

to follow the flag
through fire and hail
of arrows to the end
and silence, then
to back away, taking no bows.

Alone in my humble kitchen
after the feast, to fix myself a sandwich
and a beer and stand there

gazing into the cold box
blinded by the footlights
half forgetting—in the sudden glory—
what I came for.

WOMB RIDDLES

One of the characters on the train
was a nun. She was wrapped
in layers of gauze, open only
at the mouth.

*

 At the back of the cave
is a smaller opening, the roof so low
she can't fit through.
She presses her nose to the keyhole
and smells bread baking.
Music trickles
faintly through the mouth.

*

Let me in. Let me in, cries the wolf.
At the barred door, the pig
trembles, fat as a baby.

*

Oyster and clam.
Mussel and Scallop
come to her wedding. When she
says her valves, everyone claps.

*

Night in the sleeping car.
The scarlet drapes pulled down.
She wanders the aisle, un-
certain. Which chamber
is hers? Behind one curtain,
a couple asleep, spoon fashion.
Mother and son, the man's thumb
in his mother's mouth.

*

The gypsy child
plays a pot-bellied mandolin, music
melancholy as slavic rain. She will
surely give birth to twins.

*

A persimmon
works its way to the center of the house
and ripens. It sits in a high wing chair
at one end of the living room
and is worshipped.

*

There are two large rocks in the pot.
When you rattle the pot, the stones
knock together. Shake them. There is no soup.

*

Around this absence
we hardly assemble. A moon
not missed. It measures itself
by the size of its emptiness.

OTHER VOICES

There are voices on my line,
nameless sopranos and baritones
placing orders, telling sorrows,
importuning lovers. "It's a matter
of time," they'll say, or "Please"
or "Can't we meet?"

Sometimes they speak with accents or in
     languages
I can't identify, such beautiful
expense of breath, the heart-
words murmuring.

I've called the Company.
Men come with rubber-handled pincers,
earphones. Faces tuned
to something far away, they kneel
as if in prayer, set their
stethoscopes against the wire,

detect only the pulsing
of time, the ruffle of electrons
slipping by. My slender voices
disappear when summoned,
fading, turning, breaking now

into a minor key, like fragments
of melody in Schubert calling
from the left hand
or the right, each one absolute
in grief or joy, yet joined
and chastened by the news of others.

"SPACE ALIEN NEWSPAPER FOUND AT UFO SITE"

It's good to know we're not alone
that elsewhere in the universe
on distant planets there are others,
horned or scaly, silvery or green,
who live and suffer, work and die.

It's strange to think about them: space-age
minotaurs and griffins dressed
in jumbled features of familiar monsters,
feeler and tentacle, talon and shell. Inside
they must resemble us. Why else

would they hurl themselves over acres
of darkness and time to bring hard word
of themselves, this hapless tabloid
frisbeed like the morning paper
to a doorstep in Bolivia. Colliding

space-ships, rifted friendships, earthquakes,
poisonings— It's oddly comforting,
their news. For now when we look up
at night from the swale
of ourselves, we'll see

not emptiness and glittering
cold, but fellow-travelers who know
the constellation we are part of. Probably
they are watching us, even now, their great
antennaed heads tipped back in contemplation.

WEATHER CHANNEL

for Katharine Zadravec

I love to sit here watching
the grey screen tremble
with graphs and numbers, charmed
by temperate baritones, bland prophets
promising a better day, men in sportscoats
calling out of their sleeves: cataclysmic
eruptions, seizures of earth, the sky's
ejaculations and refusals.

My window too is a screen. Raindrops
speckle the glass, a water leopard,
frieze of tears. Some slide
down the pane, a lie
untelling itself or the lives of those
who have quit holding on.

But weather is always happening,
a harbinger pushing ahead
repeating itself like a mad dog dirge, hurricane,
flood, the brown revolutionary rivers
sweeping cities along in righteous fury.

The weather's a drama
that never ends, our life
outside the body, happening *for* us
while we sit home and watch.

Here's a veteran, home from war,
a man struck twice by lightning.
Twice his arm thrilled to the bone
and the tools he was using, hammer and cutters,
glowed like the raiments of god,
and the fence where he stood working

carried the message of him
out through barbed wire.

And once weather entered our house
through that telephone there in the corner—
wires' end. Not bolt, but fireball
it passed from hand to hand like a dog
on its rounds, then disappeared
leaving an ozone scent of burning hair
and unforeseen lightness among us.

COMMERCE

In Salzburg, Ignaz Leutgeb, merchant
of cheese, played natural horn
for Mozart who for Leutgeb
wrote three horn concerti crammed with secret
jokes and rhythms of the hunt.

Mozart was deciduous, shedding music
as the linden sheds its leaves
in colored inks, the pages
as he wrote them tossed aside
to be retrieved by Leutgeb
sheet by sheet, in instant commerce
between artist and consumer.

Mozart starved among the shadowy
staves and clefs, his warm breath
cooling in the spirit-house of music.
Leutgeb lived among the camemberts
and Limbergers, the veined and marbled blues,
the musical gruyeres and breathed
from his prodigious lungs great
globe notes, rich and runny
as the hunter's warble echoing

over hills. In fall, the fields of Austria
are filled with gold. Hounds circle on the scent
of some quick fugitive, while violins, insistent,
scratch and scratch, quick as a dog at its fleas.

CABALLOS

> *The Incas were less interested in killing the*
> *Spaniards than in killing their horses. They*
> *feared the horses more.*
> —lecture on the Spanish conquests

At first when the conquerors came,
waving shields and pikes, plumes dancing,
we thought them brilliant birds,
but when they stripped to bathe
we saw they were not gods.
Under the feathers and scales,
their genitals hung down mournful and wrinkled.
Their bodies were hairy and pale.

They brought us The Word in a black book,
tiny letters writhing like scorpions
on every page, but the horses
gave them power—Caballos
they called them—limbs striking fire
from stone as they ran. Their browsing
turned grass into flesh. Even their stools
smelled sweet.

Our gods aided us
at Cajamarca. But their gods came
in the kingly flesh. The Spaniards galloped
on their bodies as a child
riding his father's shoulders
mistakes himself for a man. Thin men

on fat horses. Fat men on thin horses.
Riding our shoulders, they made themselves lord

The first horse we killed,
we beheaded. Hung on the wall
surrounded by flowers,
the head began to weep.
It told of the sadness in flesh,
but nothing was said about the gods,
nothing to us who stood below
with offerings, burning for words.

MIRACLES

And in Orvieto we saw
among museums and palaces
two men rising in a bucket
over the brow of the gaudy
cathedral.

The bucket was yellow, of a radiance
rarely found in nature,
the carrier coupled to the crane so that
from where we watched, one man's head
was a large yellow triangle.

Up they soared, over
the medieval city, over trees and roofs
until only air was behind them,
pearly blue and brushed
with perishable clouds.

So we stood on the stones, gazing up.

If they should turn and bless us now,
the sky behind them trembling with love....
Instead, they bend to their work, as all over Italy
people are bending—pounding, welding,
wielding jackhammers and torches,

their brilliant,
anachronistic machines wedged
among the cul-de-sacs and alleyways
and raising an unholy racket, clouds
of obfuscating dust, as once

the busy monks erected in these plazas
the great beehive of faith. Only we
stand idle now, open-mouthed,
empty-handed, tourists on earth
and longing to be lifted.

QUARTET
WITH PROGRAM NOTES
BY COMPOSER

QUARTET WITH PROGRAM NOTES
BY COMPOSER

(after Gunther Schuller's Third String Quartet)

I. *Maestoso, with great intensity*

Light and shadow. Silence
and sound. An alternation
of densities.

The snake looping back
to feast on its infinite tail. Sun
rising through a veil of smoke

beyond my moving window, dark
figures shuttering past.
I'm going to New York

to talk of money. Slowing down,
speeding up. The lightning
passages, the dark

clouds bearing down. This is long,
this train called music. When will I get
to the station? How far is New York?

At last night's concert: four musicians
leaning to their instruments like acolytes
their faces incandescent, calling voices

out of tortured wood, four branches
of a wordless argument unwinding
deep in the forest of hearing.

And who will listen
when that tree falls? Will there be trees
when we are gone? Will there be music?

Which god should I invoke? Freud?
Jehovah? Clio and her mother, Memory? Mammon,
father of stores and money, of Saks-

Fifth-Avenue-silks and leathers?
Just me, alone here, Muses, singing,
Me, Me, me with my fitful wind,

my flimsy sails, thinking
When will this movement be over? How long
until silence? How far to New York?

II. *Adagio*

Movement II — Canzona.
Clear enough. Three stanzas,
three birds on a wire. At this speed,
this distance, I can't make them out.
Was it a robin, a starling?
What color and brand is it?
What is its name? — Why are you asking
so many questions? Canzona
means song, but the high note
is pain. Pain makes the brakes
screech, strangles the violin, small bones,
small bones breaking — Softly. These are
quiet pangs. A sign says "Wilmington." A tower
advertising "Bones." Two firm-fleshed ladies,
ankles crossed across the aisle,
talk handbags, labels. Going to New York
to buy. Pierre Dieux. It's lightweight.

For travel. Across the bay, a spire unfurls
an oil-black flag of smoke. The tower I build
should be tall, strong enough to bear the past:
Grandma, Lily, Rose and those
who are only stories, those
who are only names: Itche Chudje in the Pale

of Settlement, who hid in the graveyard
from Cossacks and never came home.
Pogrom. Pogrom. The name, a drum.
Cheytsippe and Sorke, the sisters,
the oldest and youngest ones,
who stayed. Guns marched with them
to the top of the hill and none
marched down again. Where are the blackbirds,
the wrens, the sturdy finches
they called *Shperl*? What was the name
of that village? What was the name of that girl?

Funeral music, please. Low tones.
One bird singing in the cemetery.
Without grief. A European bird.
Death is a species rarely sighted
here among the shops, the roofed arcades.
We lie at rest, the shaking
done, the engine quiet
in the station. Two ladies reciting
the blessing for shopping, invoking
the brands. Newspaper pages
turn and fall with a sigh like the passing
of seasons. Why are we standing here?
Where is New York? Why is she asking
so many questions? Who gave you permission
to open your mouth? (Like a bird.
Like a baby bird.) Hush, child, hush.
We will be there soon.

III. *Allegro Vivace*

Tract houses scaling past,
sidewalks spaced evenly:

  House house house house
each one crowded with stories:

When my mother was young, her mother
made Challah on Fridays, with her own
hands, braided the dough, then
covered the pan with a cloth,
as she covered the mirrors after death
until grief rose, and my mother
would carry this pan to the baker
who set their Sabbath loaf
in an oven crowded with others.

So many stories.
So many lives.

   Loaf loaf loaf loaf
in the oven crowded with others

How swiftly Philadelphia
replaces Wilmington,
America replacing Russia.
Towers burning. Men and women
turning to flame to ash.
All the gravestones
have been defaced. My brother and I
can barely stumble out a B'rucha.
Our children will light no candles.

So many stories.
So many lives.

   "Let it be forgotten, as a flower is forgotten

...as a hushed footfall
in a long forgotten snow."
My mother at my brother's
grave, reciting Teasdale,
meaning No. If any child
must die, let beauty be forgotten,

song, the old prayers. So much music
flinging itself away—

Returning from the club car now, I'm lost.
All these coaches look alike—

    Car   car   car   car
So many faces traveling

    by hundreds—face face face
going away, in trucks, in trains, can you
tell me the name of that bird?
They are leaving Russia, the twenty
children of Itche Chudje.
With their cooking pots, their many
names, their few coins wrapped in rags,
packed in the belly of the whale,
a huddle of bodies, belongings, and breath

And the days are rocking them
making them sick

    Wave   wave   wave   wave
    In a ship's hold, swarming with others

But they have escaped

    with their many names, their suitcases
stuffed with diminutives: my grandmother
Annie, Nachama; Crazy Ettel, and Edith
her namesake—called Idis or Itka
and Benjamin/Bensche; and Rose
who was Rochel and Runya—in fever
in Yiddish, in English, joking, scheming,
feuding, asking questions,
crying—

Bird-bird-bird-bird—bird—

                    flying deep
over fields of New Jersey now
where cities loom and crash like waves:
    Chester, Trenton, Newark—past
      and future
                    strain to touch—

We will meet in New York.

Coda

A closing. A seal
and a promise. A motion
curls back on itself,
a bud in a sheath,
a fist with a baby inside.
Goodbye. From cauda
the tail which the snake must grasp
so the world can replenish itself.
Goodbye. (Will there be trees
when we are gone? Will there be
music?) All I can hear
is the grinding of time,
the sound of the beast
at its supper. The pampered
wood, the tortured song —
the fruit of towering
ambition. "Schubert," he said,
"is not present" (though
he was) and I am
rising in New York
to talk of money. Who was that maiden?
And why is she leaving?

MY LIFE IN HIDING

HOW WE SPEAK TO ONE ANOTHER
WITH DREAMS

When I tell you my dream of a blue and white pitcher
the shape of a cow, I'm showing you the shape
of morning, generous cream
flowing over the lip, saying, Stay
   and I pray for continuance.

And when I tell of our two heads lifting
from long neck stems, so careful the seam
at the throat and the threat
of eruption, I'm saying
   Go slowly with me.

When I speak of the white bird flying away
and returning, and you of the woman
you lay with, rocking your hips beside me
in the dark, we speak our need for secrecy
   and for surprise:

purple haze on distant mountains, gauze around the moon,
her censored face. Each morning we lift our dreams
and hold them to the light, as at night we offer
to the other's use and keeping
   our most delicate organs. So when I dream

of a manuscript filling the shelves of a library,
spilling from rooms, I'm reading
from the archive of departures
we are building page by page of dreams,
   unfinished, endless, inexhaustible—

CURTAIN CALL

If this is the afterlife, they must be angels
wading knee-deep in golden dust
their hair and garments slightly mussed
from so much struggle.

Juliet's face still streaked with tears
Romeo, pale and bemused, they do not seem,
now that they've broken from the dream,
much more than casual acquaintances, as if
they'd stripped away their old identities
and not yet taken on the new.

Acrobats of love and hate, how readily
they threw themselves away. And yet
they rise, as we do not. Paris,
Mercutio, placid as paper dolls,
join hands across the stage
and bow— as if this bending down,
this holding on, might ask and grant
a mutual absolution. And what of us

expelled from wedding night and tomb
into this after-life of everyday, the cold
walk home, our stumbling words, the body
with its fear of pain, its dread of annihilation.
How often have we failed in love
as they did not.

WILLINGLY

Every morning when I fill the trays
we emptied yesterday, narrowing
the flow of water so the stream
runs evenly along the grid
in rippling rhythm
down one side and up the other,
as in playing a xylophone, or running
my fingers down your spine,

I think of you—and me, how far
we've come together, battles
laid to rest. And as I do for you
what you will not,
I make myself remember
that I do this for the sake
of peace and to abolish anger
like a postulant practicing self-mastery

from which love grows. Each time
I wipe the bottoms of the trays
with checkered towel and glide
to the refrigerator, sinuous as Delilah
balancing baskets on her head, voluptuous
as a saint, I make myself remember
all we took on—willingly—
when we took each other.

NEW YORK LANDSCAPE, 1908

Phillips Collection, Washington, D.C.

It is twilight now,
three years before my mother's birth
and though dusk has fallen,
one corner of the sky
is rosy with promise.
This is the earliest moment
I remember. A large star
swollen in its sac of light
hangs overhead. One by one
in windows lamps beam on.
The iron-dark tenements shine
fierce as pumpkins hoarding
interior fire. I candle
the secret image like a seed
and slumber on.

OPENING OYSTERS

With knife and glove, I am opening oysters.
Though practice hones technique, no leap
of skill will make the next one easier.
Each clenched fist lies utterly closed to me
as the last. How foolish I am

pitting my life against stones.
And force won't help. It's a matter
of attention — a secret
understanding between wrist
and thumb, inquisitor

and victim. So the skillful interrogator
abandons himself without shame to the fixed idea
of entry, seeking an opening, probing,
trying the hinge, till the knife slips in
with ease and something vulnerable

lies bare. And this may pass
as victory — though nothing more
than an encounter with the flesh
as when we walk through woods
to water in light rain and

come upon a wall of mist
immense as sky seen through tears.
It is cold, impenetrable, wet,
and when I put my tongue to it
the taste is salt.

WOMAN HASN'T SLEPT A WINK
IN THIRTY YEARS

We are all virgins here—the doll on the pillow,
the saint on the wall, neat bed
with cotton spread, taut stripes
starting straight, then veering off.
This is my all-night, every-
night chair. My ship in the desert.
And this is my cell and my sentence: never
to lose myself in that sweet river
of phantoms and fish.

What is it like, to sleep? I've forgotten
since that day I yawned
and felt the possibility slide away.
Night is a space the self
fills completely. I close my eyes.
I open them. The room stares back at me
with all its furnishings. I too
am furniture, my arms and legs
stiff as this chair's.

What does a chair think? Surely its tiny
field of energy does not rise far.
My one thought circles until
it is only a quick, mechanical
thrum. The clock-hand inches forward.
Church bells fishing catch
the hours in their nets. I push lace
curtains back, watch the clock of stars
revolving past the steeple. And this, to me,

is time: a long, dry spell, thirty years
in the desert, each dawn's provisional rain.
The birds begin their foreign dialogue.
Fernando's rooster rends the dark
with a strangled shriek, and the day
begins to jangle and lurch.
Now my neighbors rise, having journeyed far
through heaving waters. Fat and sleek
as pilchards they push off — into this world
I watch for them.

HOUSEKEEPING IN HEAVEN

There is no keeping this house without ceiling
or doors, without sills or lintel. The wind
blows through, ecstatic, tumbling our work
into feathers and scuds, undoing,
undoing. And still we vacuum,
wipe the breakfronts, tend and bake,
the sky rolled out in thin white sheets.
We shop the galaxy for bolts of light,
the steady cloth of air unwinding
curtains and handkerchiefs, blankets
and briefs. Oh, I could shine
theorems, brick by brick, plant
brilliant manifestos, borders
of diatribe and scarlet truth. Instead I'm
cleaning closets. Only the castaway
is saved. To think
how we keep dusting in this house
there is no keeping.

THE FIRES

for Myra

Meanwhile the slattern buildings along Oak Street
crouched under their dark sentence
harboring immigrant breath,
serving out their watery days
as Russian baths and synagogues until the landlords
torched them for insurance.

Amid the noise, the flying ash
and soot, we stood in flickering light
as if projected on a screen
and watched the houses of the past
undo themselves, flames
peeling back the baffles of wire
and wallpaper, exposing the secret
wounds beneath. I saw generations
turning over like the pages of a book

consumed as it was read, the silent
list of grievances at last
articulate, tall columns
of light exploding, each tongue
unfurling its fierce,
unspeakable word.

In heat, I turned to you and watched our words
break into smoke as we uttered them, our
lives, our decades shuttering past
faster than we could follow. I
shivered then and clutched my sweater
closer, while the baby, rocked
between delight and fear, lifted her hand
in a learned gesture of farewell.

                                    New Haven, 1958

THE POND

When we shine our searchbeam into the night
water, we see them hanging
in that murky soup, their arms
stretched out to us,
their bodies luminous,
before they turn
and dart away. The plucked
bass-fiddle string of love
and sorrow, silenced,
starts again, as if a current
had switched poles. Only fear
connects them with us: menace
to menace. The dual
transaction. Wet grass
on bare feet and visions
of those other grasses, groping softly
from the bottom. Yet now we leave
our clothes, dark strangers
stretched beside us on the bank
and trust our gleaming bodies
to the water with its many mouths.

TRAVELER

The gargoyles spill smooth
arcs of water from their throats
and I stand below, catching the spray
on my skin, trying to remember where I am.
What country is this? Which cathedral?

I do not remember traveling north
or south, the transitions
between illuminations.
Perhaps I traveled in a circle.
Perhaps I stayed in one place
and the world came tumbling past me
as I slept and woke.

I remember fog
and the clearings between,
each enclosing a singular gift,
a bead or a painting, a view
of hills. One holds only
the odor of garlic, another
a black leather box, with a slice
of watermelon on its lid. A slab
of pink marble inlaid with seeds.

Some days I skimmed so lightly
over the earth, scraps
and selvage of me
sloughed behind—the girl
who swam topless in Crete,
and the student of sleep,
and the one who sampled oranges—

straggler in a vast cathedral,
puzzling out the epitaph
engraved on a child's sarcophagus:
Sic tibi terra levis, May the earth
rest lightly on you.

THE DREAM OF PACKING

I am packing my possessions
clothes and papers,
the debris of seasons
strewn in four directions
like a scattered mind.

How will I fit it all in?
The red maple glowing
and dying. The yellow maple
with thinning leaves.
Richard and Bob in the kitchen
deciding at midnight
to level the icebox, Richard
with his thinning hair,
his passion for perfection,
on his knees pushing pennies
under the levelling foot
while Bob leans the length
of himself to lifting,
both of them briefly,
drunkenly happy
levelling what has listed
all these years, what in the end

will go on listing:
                        the second-hand fridge
with its sagging door,
I put that in. I put in the trees
and all of October,
the album of my childhood
with its tiny skates, white shoes
that never fit my feet.

How hard this is! The dream
is my work and the night
is passing. My Random House
sprawls unabridged on the floor.
But how can I leave
without language, my beloved
etymologies? I stuff the dictionary in.
At last the rooms are bare of all
that housed me here —

except for scars on the floor
where the furniture
clawed its way free, and ghosts
of pictures on the wall, exhausted
shadows, pale as dawn
in windows. Now I am ready. Now
I can open my eyes.

MY LIFE IN HIDING

My life in hiding
is not unlike your own.
Each morning, I clap a tame face
over my wild one, dress as you dress,
train my gestures to resemble yours.

Time touches me,
brushing my skin. Money
slides through my hands.
Eggs siphon through my body,
sand through glass.

There are days when nothing happens,
evenings when the winter sun
turns the sky to a city in flames.
Sometimes I speak to myself
and a stranger answers.

When the child began to grow inside me,
clambering from deeper into lighter shade,
to crown from hiding

into hiding, I saw how camouflage
contains disclosure, how each unveiling
draws us

into deeper disguise. And so I rise
from caves of wrath to live
as one of you, a woman wrapped
in silence, bearing alive
my buried name.

AFTERWORD

When Bernardine Dohrn was apprehended after years living underground, she remarked to the press, "I'm surprised I wasn't found sooner." That small remark, dashing my romantic notion of resistance, provoked the title poem of this collection.

It's been curious for me, putting this book together, to notice echoes of political discourse creeping into my work. Curious, because I've never had much affection for political rhetoric, for movements and "isms." Ideological thinking, comforting as it must be to the converted, has always struck me as a form of violence against the richness of individual experience, the promise (and terror) of uncertainty—which is why poems which start out too firmly wedded to a fixed agenda so often end up short-cutting truth in favor of "right opinion." To live with metaphor is to dwell, as Dickinson reminds us, "in Possibility" —a world without conclusion.

When I was in graduate school studying German literature, one of the things that charmed me about Bertolt Brecht was the way he would start out, with best intentions, to write plays that would be "politically correct," then veer off, dangerously and thrillingly, in other directions. He wanted to be a good soldier for his cause, but he had difficulty marching in step. Political discourse, in the hands of an artist like Brecht, tends to transcend utilitarian purposes, to expand in heretical directions. What we experience as reality is too complex, too wildly paradoxical to lend itself neatly to doctrine, and it is to the perplexing, largely unarticulated state of consciousness that a writer owes primary allegiance.

The politics I grew up with was that of the Old Left: New York, secular, Jewish, socialist, unionist. No one I knew in my childhood ever knowingly crossed a picket line or voted Republican. My grandfather went devoutly to *schul*, and my grandmother took her babies to hear Eugene V. Debs. One of my earliest memories is of my parents by the radio, weeping when Roosevelt died.

That world has largely vanished, and the terms of the old debate, with all the irony of loss, are now available —can be appropriated, if we will—for metaphor. If the old political faith seems, at this juncture, exhausted, the emotional content behind it—with its drama of repression, deprivation, liberation, and revolution—remains valid as ever on a personal level. Our sense of self is always under siege from what is outside: not just death, loss, the traditional enemies, but the whole fabric of the public world which presses in upon us so insistently and so confusingly. As individuals, we struggle to preserve ourselves by "pressing back", (in Stevens' words), creating spaces where private reality can survive and prosper in the face of that which threatens to annihilate it. Imagination belongs always to the Underground.

But all such explanations are very much after-the-fact. When I wrote these poems I was feeling my way like a blind woman, brick by brick, stone by stone along the streets of a strange, yet familiar city.

for Nicki
and my good friend
Ken Shedd

BRUCE BOND

The Anteroom of
Paradise

BRUCE BOND was born in 1954 in Pasadena California. He received a BA in English from Pomona College, an MA in English from Claremont Graduate School, and an MA in music performance from the Lamont School of Music. After working for several years as a classical and jazz guitarist, he earned a PhD in English from the University of Denver. His collections of poetry include a chapbook *The Ivory Hours* (Heatherstone Press) and a full-length collection *Independence Days* (Robert Gross Award, Woodley Press). He has been a Scholar at the Bread Loaf Writers' Conference, a Fellow at the Virginia Center for the Creative Arts, and a professor of English at the University of Kansas and Lock Haven University. Presently he lives with his wife on the Susquehanna River in central Pennsylvania.

CONTENTS

I.

Planetarium	8
The Ivory Hours	9
Tattoo	11
Katherine's Eye	12
Gallery of Rivers	14
The Art of Memory: Neighborhoods	15
Chinatown	16
Still Life with Lemons	18

II.

Kurt Weill	20
Alban Berg	21
Schoenberg	22
Mahler: *Kindertotenlieder*	23
Shostakovich	24
Webern	25
Varese	26
Stravinsky	27
Bartok	28
Hugo Wolf	29
The Final Days of Robert Schumann	30
Ravel	31
Bach's Idiot Son	32
Satie	33
Ives	34
Piano	35
Messiaen	36
Emigrant's Song	37

III.

Winter's Apprentice   40
Hospice   42
Visitation   43
The White Field   44
Prayer   45
Elegy   46
The Anteroom of Paradise   47
    1. Vermeer: The Maidservant
    2. Matisse: The Red Studio
    3. Cezanne: Apples and Oranges
    4. Whistler: The White Girl
    5. Van Gogh: The Night Café
Paradise Carnival   51

AFTERWORD   54

I.

PLANETARIUM

As the mobile of planets wheeled over my crib,
their shadows darkened the yellow walls,

a ripening pear. My mother frowned
tenderly like a mirror, touched

her fingers to her nipple, placing there
the word *milk*, then took her hand away.

The syllable drifted to the floor of my body,
a shiny lure swivelling through the dark—

my first imagination of need. A toy piano
played lullabies on its metal teeth.

When my mother leaned down to kiss me,
she pressed her face on the pad of my silence;

then she withdrew, jostling the planets.
That night, my parents slept lightly. The sky

lay wind-stripped and polished to its tar.
When I spoke, they imagined themselves

emerging in my first words; like children,
they lit up at the names they were given.

THE IVORY HOURS

Dangling her legs from the piano bench,
my daughter balances wooden matches

on the backs of her hands.
She descends the white stairs of C,

her fingers carefully entering rooms,
the silence of their blind dates.

Feeling my presence, she falters,
curses herself.

It's always too soon to tell
how much rehearsal is enough,

as though the hours ahead were a tall glass
we save for a guest.

Most of us play banquets
and memorials, church weddings for near

strangers. We light up successive nights
in practice rooms, rows of them,

cool, white as distant calendar days.
I follow their corridors through the muted

clash of neighboring keys
to the bare calendar room

where my daughter spreads her music.
There are no windows, only the mindfulness

of her spinet singing into the outer wall.
A match falls in her lap.

She has been rehearsing this piece
for what seems an eternity now.

It is complex as apricots
and pheasant, the Arabic tongue,

the way they darken in our mouths
until we wake with a trace of ourselves

dreaming in their terms.
Once in a great while she leans

on a chord: rain breaks the straw
back of August. As the water ribbons

off the bones of her hands, she hears boys
outside, the clack of their bats

as they gather them up. They are running
for the trees, drenched and laughing.

TATTOOS

We imagined them
as shell-shock and rice-wine
surfacing on Asian nights.
My mother told us not to stare,
though his arms were the typhoid streets.
He would have loved them for life,
the women with diminutive names
and strong hands needled
into his skin: their high-heeled
initials, the blue florets.
I see him in the showers
by the city pool, lathering up
the thorns on his thigh.
Foam streams over his shoulders,
the broken skiff blazing
into his chest. And where
there's fire, the thin fury
of hair. As each blue cell
flakes off, the next comes up
blue, faithful, as though
the color were his gene's amnesia,
and marriageable women
would shun him now for fear
their children would be tough
and blue, the fool thicket
of roses fixing its stale kiss
on their thighs, their nipples.
They would wear their family's
blue, recurrent dream, a cold
fire surfacing between them.

KATHERINE'S EYE

It's the faithfulness that fools us,
how its fine red vein
slips under the living seam.

When Katherine lost her glass eye
in the deep-end of her uncle's pool,
her brothers scouted the blue

floor, excited and horrified,
listening for its tap and roll.
If you find yourself staring now,

half-forgetting, unsure
which is which, you are proof
of the attention it draws

into its glass bowl
like a silvery helix of fish.
We cannot feel how her shade

thickens to the one side,
which half chills
slightly in the winter.

The two move with the parallel ease
of synchronized swimmers.
They are beautiful sisters

who hide whatever differences
they feel. When she looks through
the partial-light across her pillow

into her lover's eyes,
her one pupil grows dark
and large as the room itself.

It's been years, and he is still
curious. The glass eye
beckons him from its foreign places

like a postcard of the planet
earth. It's the color
that paradise borrows from our

better days, glass-
blue, a window in the body
that has no other side.

GALLERY OF RIVERS

In your watercolors of Texas, a mosquito floats
in a glass of milk. Hot light pours
through the memoirs of trees,
imagining how the street-tar softens
or the vaguely bruised shade of brick.

The scene lays down its magnificent burden
of affection, having come so far,
and appeals to us, the way lovers
appeal to each other's silence.
Morning sun hurls across the widest day of the year.

When I look in your breezeways,
their sparse stories, the abundance
of white, it's Sunday.
No one dies or gets married:
I cannot know your stories, where to begin,

how they lead like one story
through the walls of a summer
boathouse, its warm lock. This morning
you call me back to bed, stretch your legs.
We are slipping words inside each other's words,

turning against the solace of rivers,
the belief that we never step in the same
word twice, the same story, the same
hot Texas street. Your story's horizon
wavers in the head as though the very air

resists us: where the river thickens
and bends, a girl sketches in the mud
with a stick. Above her the August afternoon
nearly pauses in its canvas, then draws
away, broad, white, refusing to be filled.

THE ART OF MEMORY: NEIGHBORHOODS

Giordano Bruno lived in all twenty-four rooms.
He made an art of remembering each.
In the first, he kept stone paths
and creek beds. The second—
fireflies, waterspiders.
And so it went on through the hours
he housed in close quarters
with a choice of chairs and a view.
In an Inquisition prison cell,
woods bloomed because he put them there.
He couldn't remove them, any more
than swallow what he said and walk away.

My wife sleeps with me.
We spend our nights in different houses.
I dream of breaking down the door
into her smoldering room.
Inside every room is another room,
a word sheathed in a word.
My love is never small enough.
I look up from my finger in books
and ask her the origins
of *tolerance* and *passion*.
Some mornings, I rub the smoke
from my eyes beside closed windows,
magazines, her there waking slowly.

Our neighbors decided on a white wedding
at St. Mary's Basilica downtown.
I'd forgotten what it was like:
the smell of wax, tendinous vaults
holding the large silence into place.
They ate bread and knew themselves
as each other in Christ,

the something lost in translation.
The bride's vows were so soft
I got the mere drift of it
from the movement of her lips.
Cameras flashed from every angle as they kissed.

CHINATOWN

It's hot July, the year of the monkey,
and the paper lanterns hang out their hopes

for the furlough of a north wind.
People rise from the subway stairs

and fan out, skirting past the floating
crap-game, window-gates, the smell

of tangerines and marijuana.
A man steps under the brash marquee

crackling as it scrawls its one promise
always upward away from the street—

and off, then up again, a pink highball
balancing briefly on the spike heel of light.

A girl walks a cat on a string.

Inside the stripper reaches through her legs
to stroke the remaining blue scarf,

to pull it aside like a doll-house curtain:
the future is always two places;

as the broad light of fortune sets
in one, it rises in the other.

A boy blows into his dice.

Between the black booths that flirt
with never being there, the stripper

searches for the occasional
enthusiast and slides her looks

like a warm towel around him and away.
She folds her dollars carefully

into her belt, as though they too
were flesh. A man offers up

a slow stream of them, singles
in a gradual strip-tease

of his own, his money going
where he won't, a kiss

blown through the vines of smoke,
a madrigal of good rain that floats

to the north and cannot fall.

STILL LIFE WITH LEMONS

By the lemon grove, you hold your ice
in the light of an empty glass:
I stand in your photograph, apprenticed
to your absence, your flesh, the porous
field stitched in your blouse. The near past
is a fist of seeds. We have buried our names
in each other, stained our tongues in the clear ink.

I pace from spool to spool of ink.
The museum shadow slips its ice
down the yellow hill. I hold you under the names
of trees—your tongue, a gloss
to a basket of lemons; our past
is a penniless apprentice.
It sleeps buried in a ledger, these porous

days. I love your letters. Our porous
lives dip into the ink
of immediate nights. Real hands apprentice
us to these immediate dreams: ice-
bright fingers over opulent platters, a past
of creams and berries, affectionate names
on our tongues. Our mouths are shallow glasses.

I am sending you this photograph, this glass
party that will not smear. You can see us
breathing, welling up with each other's names.
My eye is a tentacle of ink.
I am thin, apprenticed
to your real hands. We eat the past
and are eaten—your tongue, a lemon, a flare of ice.

II.

KURT WEILL

In the brick shade, a blind man sang.
His monkey raised its bent cup,
danced to the concertina.
Another man kept time with a cane.

When butter soared to a hundred
thousand marks a pound, Kurt Weill
considered his songs practical: children
sang them, holding each
precarious note like a small nail.

Just what his tattered dances changed
is unclear. Friends played them
in their heads like a knowledge
that something was wrong
but never unlovely.

Fog slid under the bridge.
Through his window overlooking the square,
he could hear the streetmusic,
its hoarse reeds and leaky bellows.

By this hour, the phrases were breathing
more heavily: like sleep, he thought,
something we can use.

ALBAN BERG

After the great war, his opera singers wandered
into the dissonance of forest ponds.
He loved the way the violins huddled
into clusters, how his heroine
dangled from the black thread of her voice.

But in the blackest times, he thought,
the music we hear turns white again:
the way the city whitens in the winter,
the way a child's voice is white
as he rocks his fantastic horse;

it was Carnival, 1933:
an Aryan winter blew through the ears
of porticos in hoarse, white drifts.
A man swept his steps in the snow, turned back
to see them filling up again.

As Berg's taxi swerved through the heart
of Munich, it sputtered over the ice and stalled.
Across the street, boys cursed a tailor shop.
A window broke; a glittering anthem
stumbled out of the bright cafe, a shredded

parade where joy rained in bits of paper
and loud men toppled to the snow, laughing.
The blizzard thickened over his windshield,
and he drew his cape shut like a curtain
between the world and a world more dark, more sweet.

SCHOENBERG

He kept his unfinished work under a bust of Bach.
The pool of its shadow lengthened across his blotter.

His music began in idleness with a view
of the sundial, its pinned hand. He would be anything

but another Bach, have anything but a stone's
allegiance, its gravity. Day loitered from window

to window as he counted the panes of glass and laughed.
Thirteen. He knew he would die that day, a healthy man

at seventy-six. Seven, six: thirteen. To him at least,
it all added up. The clock startled him with its

small bell.
In the yard, his wife praised the dog for doing nothing.

She longed for her husband's superstition to pass
with the day. The neighbors laughed with a guest.

Was this what he was to become—sound,
the long pull on a cigarette exhaled over the back

of a darkening neighborhood? He waited
for the shapes of his room to merge, music

on a wire stand, braided wicker, the unmeasured
tapping of levolor blinds: rows of empty staves.

MAHLER: *KINDERTOTENLIEDER*

They have just gone out for a long walk.
It would take months to find land secluded enough.

In the pleated seats of a private railcar,
he made plans, rough lines pencilled into the Alps.

A book about dead children lay on a blanket in his lap.

He moved in with his grand piano wheeled to the French doors
and the unfinished painting of a girl's back. The lake

she watched was large and cold. He played Bruckner,
flattened his hair with a broad palm. With his book

about children wired open on a stand, he copied its lines
onto a sheet of music: *they have just gone out for a long walk.*

The following summer, he dined with a new wife half his age,
pulled open a second bottle of wine. Floors lay exposed

for the live sound of it. She slipped off his glasses
as he played what his hands would remember.

Her back to the lake, she felt their child move.

SHOSTAKOVICH

The cinema piano was badly out of tune.
No matter. From the back, the ping
of an empty bottle. The young Dmitri played on.

His, he thought, was the soul of the silent
boy, the comrade above who freed their flag
from pale hands, then tripped on enemy fire.

Later, Dmitri made it home through the cold.
Even darkness was white this time of year.
He put his faith in the future, emptied his hand

into his mother's: two rubles and a kopeck.
"Your father would have been proud," she said.
As she fussed with his hair, he pocketed

his fingers, hid the waver of his pride
in the private beginnings of a solo piece,
a hymn, perhaps, to liberty.

WEBERN

With me, things never turn out as I
wish, but as is ordained for me—
as I must. —Anton Webern

It was his job to be careful,
proofreading Wagner
in a government office.

He watched the skylight in its high ceiling.
When lights blackened
over Vienna, bombers descended,

pitch on long ropes. He committed
fugues to memory on a sleeping-car
rattling back to Salzburg.

Sheltered inside a small town
and chamber suite, he pieced together
a crab canon, a cat's cradle

reversing itself in his hands.
Voices cadenced on perfect
fifths, the opened loops of string.

He played records—Schoenberg,
Ockeghem—his shelves and chairs
arranged into places he expected

in the dark. Unaware of the time,
he stepped out into the post-war
curfew for a smoke.

VARESE

He wrote little during the war, mostly listened.
Dust settled on Japan.
                    Renovated railcars
on bridges from Queens threw sparks
into the black water. He took risks, long walks,
moved through crowd noise like a radio needle.

Construction crews blasted rotten buildings,
their fisted clouds like great names vanishing
over the Hudson. Streets emptied their pockets
into large, unfurnished rooms.
                      He composed
entire nights, splicing the rubble, worked
lotions into his aching hands. All wars,
he thought, are cities flowing into cities.

STRAVINSKY

Between the Russian cities, snow-mice
scoured the empty silos.
He squeaked his lenses with a scarf.
Black limbs sparked in the sun.

Music is powerless, he thought,
to express anything. It's never happy
or sad, but scatters brightly
through the wide spaces in our talk.

Where Poland burrowed its white head
into scrawls of border-wire,
finches chirped, shook
the dry powder from their backs.

It's understandable,
how he would make us into closer listeners,
set fire to nothing
but the ball of mist overhead.

When the war broke, he boarded a train
for the Swiss Alps. St. Petersburg
flared into drifts behind him.
As he slept, his passacaglia lay

pinned under an empty glass.
He saw cities, the flashing dome:

a peasant in a book of Russian tales
pieced together his clarinet;
a runaway soldier from Pinsk
pressed his red fingers
to the violin, telling stories.

BARTOK

What is the best way for a composer to reap the full benefits of his studies in peasant music? It is to assimilate the idiom of peasant music so completely that he is able to forget all about it and use it as his musical mother tongue.
—*Bela Bartok*

I. Budapest (1920)

The day Rumania fell
below the Hungarian border, he was called
a traitor for his work. His record needle

plowed through the gravel of white noise,
black vinyl, a peasant's bagatelle.

Holding his ear to the phonograph bell,
he closed his eyes and listened through the hiss:
long black skirts spreading in the mountain fog.

I. The Bronx

Solos mainly. Ever since they sold the upright, he
and his wife boxed their music for four hands. Withdrawing
deep into the small hours, he slouched over a baby grand

waiting to play. As they watched movies from the homeland,
tanks rolled soundlessly from one reel to the next.

It was 1942. His letters unanswered,
the silence from Hungary curled into his mouth
like a mother tongue.

HUGO WOLF

He arrived at the asylum in a velvet jacket.
"Mahler is discharged. I hold the appointment now."
A nurse met the carriage and led him
with promises of better days to the door.

He re-entered the confusion of quiet rooms
and demanded an explanation. Statues
mocked him. He swore his next song
would lacerate the nerves in a block of marble.

He dragged them out of bed to the upright
and rooted his chords in the black keys.
Music, he thought, is the vampire of words.
That fall, he grew rat-eyed and lean.

Then the snows came. He stared at the white keys
unable to remember his convalescent's ode.
Rummaging the quiet, he kept his pieces
brief for the satisfaction
of closing them in his hands like books.

THE FINAL DAYS OF ROBERT SCHUMANN

My ear is a violin
  with one white string.

  It chills the water
standing in its glass,
  shivers in the dark,
   and will not sleep.

So too, the stories.
  My father stared over
   the river-bridge and lived

to die naturally,
  a stone polished
   with inarticulate grief.
It knocks in my piano.

  So too, my sister's arms,
   feet—more stones,
their luster drained
  by a family weakness.

  What is it that wrings
a madwoman's body
  in its grip? Night

descends the spiral staircase
  in our palms
   leaving a trail of wet beads.

My hands are birds that know
  north from south.
   The new land is what
their wings remember.

Tell me
   these aren't my father's dreams.
This isn't my father's violin.
   The wind is not the impossible

tuning of the world.
   When it rains,
I am watching what it is
   that rains:

   my father leads me to the river's
edge, a white note
   tossing in his lamp.

RAVEL

It started with insomnia. His hand tore
the page it turned. He coaxed his fingers

to play the notes he couldn't name. Days fled
the failing tissue like refugees into a land

of many tongues, a ganglia of bare trees bending
in music he couldn't place. He craved a nap,

a sandwich, a medical miracle—swore
his opus was incomplete. So little of him left.

BACH'S IDIOT SON

He plunks the fat string
on his father's gamba
and watches the sound
blur like a bee's wing:

how lucky to be alive,
to have slipped out somewhere
between stillbirth
and genius, to arrive

here in stubborn wonder
and neglect by a dry pot
in the winter-light.
In a near room, his father

plays the virginal—a ground
bass for the glory of God.
The music says that heaven exists.
The boy hears his own sound

vanish into his father's.
So too, the father's music
vanishes into the boy's:
his spoon and platter.

The clattering says that stars
listen: take me to the house
of doors and colors, lift me
over the carriage stair.

Lord give me talented sons,
the father thinks,
but then this is God's child,
the art of faith comes

easily to him. The father buries
himself in a broad chorale.
And all across Leipzig, the idiot
children are glad and needy.

SATIE

In the morning hair
of trees, a nightingale
with a toothache spirits
a bachelor on his insouciant
stagger up the boulevard.

The air is no less
than months behind in its rent,
but whistles with the thin man,
an annoyance of chablis
on its breath. After all,
he accepted the commission,
once they conceded to pay
him less. The less of him,
the less to forget. Pride,
he thought, is painfully
constipating: let those
who choose to ignore him
hang from their intestines.

Overhead, nuts fall.
The squirrels are in bloom.

IVES

*Why can't music go out in the same way it comes in to
man, without having to crawl over a fence of sounds,
thoraxes, catguts, wire, wood and brass.*
                                        —Charles Ives

Cars blared in the wet street.
  He refused to go. The concert première
lagged fifty-some years behind.
  In a porous room, top-floor,
he tinkered at the radio:

filaments of birdsong snarled in thickets.
  He heard the congregation rumble
to its feet, high and teetering voices singing
  Watchman, tell us of the night.

The train clattering on its stilts
  tunnelled into its own chord.
Dissonance, he thought, makes room for us.
  It levels fences, waters the plains,
draws us out in forever deflating fuses,
  hushed bleachers tracking a fly.

Lowering the radio, he listened
  for the likes of two brass bands,
one from the past, the other future:

*why can't we go out in the same way
  we come in—thoraxes,
catguts, wires and brass dropped
  through both our tattered pockets,
two boys clacking their sticks
  on the pickets, receding from either ear.*

He listened as his cat skittered
a cork over the floor. Children ran
in the scant rain. He felt light, mute.

PIANO

As Clara leafed through her husband's
compositions in her lap,

his *Carnival, The Wild Horseman,*
quavers bound in a florid cursive

down one staff to the next, from one hand
to another, hardly breathing,

she fingered the passages on her knee
and listened to the sound they made.

She looked up, alone with the kind of quiet
rooms have after a banquet.

Beside her, a ravaged plate, hydrangea and lilies,
flushed, drugged, bruised like plums,

the olive pit still clinging to its meat.
A page slipped to the floor.

In another room, a tap dripped into its pan
with a staggered gait, lame and tireless,

never farther than a room away, never near.
She sipped iced coffee, black, sweet.

On the side of her porcelain cup,
a pianist suspended his hands over the keys,

his head tilted to one side,
listening to the music,

its infinite variety.
He never could touch the piano—

like a box inside a lover's eye,
a spare blue shape that curved away.

MESSIAEN

The day he arrived at the stalag, he stood for hours
naked in the heat. Above him, the birds
braided their paths in a Mobius strip.

He'd never known such hunger. Keeping his watch,
the guards gave back his bag of scores: Schumann,
Bach—the dead, he thought, made flesh in song.

He told himself hunger would be his blessing. It vivified
the world: the night the aurora borealis unfurled, he saw
the music he'd been hearing. By flashlight, he bored

a hole through the core of night conceiving
a quartet for the end of time. Each note perched
on the fence of its clef, anxious to assume

the air. This was his dream. That he would pass
like sound through barbed gates into an abyss of birds.
As he wrote, the bones of his hand floated to the surface.

EMIGRANT'S SONG

Over the hills in Veteran's Park,
the way the lanes of small flags
flutter in place like fish.

The way their colors stream
along the tidal floor.
The way butterflies migrate

in yellow hordes
over the factory waters of the Kaw.
The way our deepest allegiances

know they die. How we stand floating
on the shadows of our feet:
music justifies us.

It folds its black coat as we fold ours
and leads us past bread lines
into memorial gardens.

It weaves its milk in our mother's
voice, the physical current of our trust.
Music stares back in poor time

exposures of dim vestries,
glass-bottom boats swaying
over sunken hills, sea-leaves,

St. Jerome's hands flickering into flame.

Emily's voice is like this,
wavering visibly in her throat
on sweltering days in Whittier, California.

Hypnotic fans loosen her hair
from its funeral veil.
She brushes a fly from her hymnal.

Music justifies her. It draws out
her sympathy for ideas,
for words like *light*,

the saintly bodies in a blaze
of flags, for grace that bends
under the eyes of emigrants

on crowded decks gliding into harbor.
It slips from her throat like the voice
of someone talking in her sleep,

past help, past disbelief.

III.

WINTER'S APPRENTICE

The praying mantis tilts
its brittle head, serrates a leaf
with its pincers, swallows—
the bead of its brain so taut
there's no thinking back.
It simply moves
like the sound of a tree falling
apart. Leaning down
into its mirrored eye,
we enter the world
it sees. Here is a new order
of wildness, neither hungry
nor mad, a dry rasp,
the afterlife of leaves.

These November nights, wind
rattles the luminous cube
of our house. I see more
of my family when the weather is bad.
Last night my daughter broke
into a fever. She rehearsed
old age, shook the snowing
crystal in her hands.
It was suddenly rare:
a Polish churchyard locked
in a sea-turtle's egg.
She shook it again, firmly,
held the cold glass to her ear.

As the first snow turns black
on the seminary parking lot,
I back my father's blue Ford
through the warmth of its exhaust.

I am a string of occasions
gathered into my father's
memory. My daughter and I
enter St. Thomas Cathedral,
its high pediment a shoreline
suspended over the astonished
tide of fluting and wax.
What we offer the dead
is guesswork, larkspur,
violets: our blessings.
We choose our seats and imagine
the weather, watch daylight
swell on the windows,
the aureoled faces there.
Heaven is a city:
it has its own parks
and cafes, its own stone plaza
under the lemon trees,
its own hospital where the nurses
are slightly kinder and wiser.
And when fathers die there,
they do not look away
from their sons but ascend
to yet another heaven. My daughter
laces her palms together:
here's the church, here's
the steeple, open the door;
and we are fingers
on God's two human hands.
Under a blue scarf, a woman
prays, her palms leaning
on the mirrors of each other.

HOSPICE

Tom heals best in the dreamless portion
where nerves are quiet trees in winter.

He opens his eyes in the middle of the night
and feels better. He has nothing left:

no maps of the way back, no green cry
of wild parrots. Morning sleep

carries in its steaming kettle
of images—little for the healing.

As his body shrinks, loses hair
and telephone numbers, he grows heavy,

sleeps with always more days,
a scattering of powerless boats.

He longs to know what it is to be taken in
by absence, how to drop the soul's dime

in the fountain of his body.
By the window in a Mexican hospital,

he rolls his head in its oarlock,
rows afraid for the empty islands.

Over the dark water, the drunken
tavern flickers, full of a language.

VISITATION

I do not know how to talk to a dying man
about paradise. For weeks your absence

goes out in straight lines over the trees
and curves. It refuses to leave

completely or let me near.
I walk to the window, and there it is:

the great blue heron, vigilant, blind
to itself, the yellow sequin of its eye

stitched to the slightest movement.
It dips its slender beak, drinks,

wades into the ice-green water,
lifting the slow brambles of its feet.

And when it takes its fish, strikes fast
at the mirror, it's as though

something takes the water as well.
These nights I am angry in my sleep.

You always had more faith.
You wake in a sweat, weak, thin as rain,

look out from your remembering body:
there is no end to your story, no return.

I blame the straight lines, how they lie down
on heart monitors, spear through the dark cries of fish.

THE WHITE FIELD

for Wray (—1982)

Say we are no longer in the future.
We are sitting on your threadbare sofa,
you salting your red drink.

Say too the music snows dryly
through the wide spaces
in our talk: out of the white field
an iron wheel rolls and exhausts itself in the powder:

it's our last evening.
Naturally we cannot know it as our last.
That will be my future,
and you are no longer there.

This frees you to leave your thought
unfinished, to move about
with unconscious joy.

Knowing what I will know, I would save you,
change your plans,
or try as people try, worry you
with my foolishness.

PRAYER

Little by little, I have learned to live
on honeydew and cigarettes.

It has nothing to do with forgetting:
I know about the past, forgave my parents

my disappointment, repeating forgiveness
till these lips took it over like a prayer.

I long to be a letter to paradise—
my body, thin and given, a kind word,

as though it were heaven's desire
for me to vanish into the charity

and horror of God's white hands.
I have waited in the dark, lit

by the whorish light of African fish:
propane-blue parachutes

shredded in the trees. There's always
a black, diaphanous one—swallowing.

I used to fear I would fall through
the mouth of our toilet.

When my mother strapped me to the seat,
I squirmed like a monkey astronaut.

Catherine of Siena, you understand
what a mother does to her child

When she needs to take away the milk.
She puts something bitter there.

No bitterness tonight. I love this room.
Floating in the bath, these hands

break their long, maternal lease;
they slip through heaven's needle.

ELEGY

for Weldon Kees

This is the Golden Gate, the abandoned car,
the red mist that sinks after a great storm.
This is the one flame on its stem,
spinning. We cannot know where
your armadillos wandered, why your chorus
drifted flat and quit, how fares
your dear and fatalist parrot Boris.
You of course were wrong: there are
no public endings. Only unfinished,
private things. You floated the smile
of a bather in your good hand—frail,
bright, a denial of seasons. The world,
you said, is always waiting outside
like a bulldog or a sad valise.
To be involved then was to be worldless,
more lost than losing, a sky plunging into the sky.

THE ANTEROOM OF PARADISE

1. Vermeer: The Maidservant

Always we return to milk braiding
as it pours. Here the room
convenes like pigeons, faithful,
the stones of bread in Puritan
light—one window, one shade—
her shoulders massive and slack:
a church bell tilting
her gaze into the bowl.

It's no place we know,
only one we remember badly,
the fired blue porcelain,
steadfast among us, a bold
crease in her wimpled scarf.
Like the dead, she is generous
with her time, even tempered
as milk, magnolias blooming
in a jar in Pennsylvania.
Her hands needn't budge.
If they did, the slender
cord of milk might break

the illusion of all things
measured together, the lucid
pantry where nothing moves
but the consideration of loaves
for each other, basketry
pegged at the angle of her head,
the goodness of bowls draining themselves.

*

Our daughter waits outside
the picture as though less
alive for the slightest moving.
In the near quiet of our house,
the thermostat fires its row of gas.
Nothing she hesitates to do
snaps the trance of the dead
things rearranged on shelves,
photographs of church weddings,
our young mothers in white.

By the barn out the only window,
a checkered ball pauses over
the leaves on its way to a girl.

2. Matisse: The Red Studio

Without the slant of his paintings,
there would be no implication
of a second wall. His red easel
would shiver in a violent dream.

But their frames have folded his room
into a cube, a sauna where sunburnt nudes
water their backs and increase
the radiance which is everywhere,
they and a few privileged things:
slim crayons, the empty glass.

No windows here, no doors, no shade.
"In order to paint," he said,
"I need to remain for several days
in the same state of mind."

When the steeple on Saint Michelle's
caved into flames,
he was forty-five, too old to fight

or think his art could stand
between history and its victims.

From the same chair in Morocco,
he watched his women ripen
into oranges under the constant sun.
It's a lot to ask in a troubled time,
to be taken in, the loyal osmosis
of sunlight through our closed eyes.

3. Cézanne: Apples and Oranges

Your postcard came from the sanitarium,
a picture, you said, hung neglected
in the foyer. By whom, you didn't say,
or how you came to know this.

Apples and oranges: like most things,
we're taught there's no comparison,
no good reason not to choose one.

They take their refuge in twisted sheets,
the compote uneasy as it cranes its neck,
airborne billiards of fruit which swear

allegiance to no one. You once said you know
only two things: everything resembles
everything else, and nothing resembles

anything. Apples the color of oranges,
the succulent rose on a chilled pitcher,
each discretely becoming one another,

mutually withdrawn. Beneath plush crevices,
they slip us paradise brochures, brilliant
as leaves, where heroes fail and shuffle
their pages of shade, considering the options.

4. Whistler: The White Girl

Not yet the bearskin
rug with its head,
or the brown glass
of her eyes there,
posed clover, dropped,
marigolds abused
as plums. Not
yet the rough
stitch of carpetflowers,
a garden startled
through bathroom glass.
For first there is
the white girl, even
before the fallen
hair or failed
shoulder, the white
dominion she holds
in an old place:
her lily, the hand,
her finely sutured
sleeves in a den
between linen walls
where women study drapes
to learn the graces
of crossing such
rooms without betrayal.

5. Van Gogh: The Night Café

They come for the comfort
of abandoned chairs. Nowhere
else is the drink cheap

or the lanterns lit
with bees. Lovers choose
the furthest corner,

not bothering to slip off
their hats. Looking this way,
a man waits for a partner

at pool—the felt, a fine
layer of algae. He's the only
one here in a summer suit,

lambent white: his coat
attracts a moth or two.
In the company of chairs,

he stands between the pool
table and a cleared booth:
one hand at his hip,

ready: the other napping
in his pocket's linen.
He feels at his best this late

when tentativeness passes
for nonchalance, and the room,
radiant as a sugar cube,

sweetens what the night is.
From its carafe,
a bouquet looks out

amazed at the room's likeness
to day. Thin, unreliable,
a light blue table holds up

the head of a sleeping man.
12:10:
already it's tomorrow.

PARADISE CARNIVAL

Stormy nights, the snow blazes in my television:
I bury my insomnia in the light
of its winter hills, the late news,
girls strapped in ambulance trolleys.
Most of what I know I forget. It works
the way a car works in our hands,
the radio on. A body on its walk home:

I am listening to a shrill calliope
at the Paradise Carnival. My father
straps his trembling son in his lap.
The roller-coaster locks and glides
upward through its scaffolding,
rounds its precipice where it pauses,
a boat atop the sunken city lights.

Children look up through the water
in envy. The boat casts off plunging
into screams of joy, a garish meal
swallowed by the mouth of an Alpine cave.
I have dreamt of this mountain every night
for a week now. I wake in a sweat,
unclench the boat from my jaw.

I love my work but dread the long drive
in winter, chevrolets sunk and abandoned in the snow.
The highway eats the better fifth
of my days. I use the time to worry
about my son sparring in mirrors,
punishing crickets with lighter fluid,
how he sits in front of the speeding cars
on televisions, socks his buddies
a little too hard with the joy he feels.

It's always been my ambition to live
another life. I always wanted to write
erotic letters to the world, to tell
the secrets that get untold:
under a blanket in the sun, the world
rereads the passages it finds
less perfect. They dying never go
to paradise. Only the dead.

So the children are delivered.
Their mothers are lovely
and shunned, made strange and ready
for the child's departure, the plunge
into the body of light.
The boy who grows up to be my son rises
in our father's boat.

AFTERWORD

I like to think this book picks up where my last book left off—with a birth, a coming into language, and so a coming into a world we name even as it name us. The inception of words has long been a source of wonder for me, implying as it does our simultaneous distancing from and bonding with the world. The rooms throughout this volume provided me with a way of talking about forms of separation, of shelter and exclusion. But like Ive's apartment, the rooms here are "porous." They are anterooms—made livable by the amorous imagination that inhabits them.

I am attracted to poems that are amorous in the largest sense, poems which seduce, not necessarily by way of their sensuousness, but by seeming to listen as they speak, conceal as they reveal. There's a disturbing section in Eliot's "Burnt Norton," the meditational pivot in the poem where he says, "Desire itself is movement/ Not in itself desirable." The lines would be personally more convincing if people were limited to one desire at a time, if we were not self-contradictory. Fact is, it's difficult for me to imagine desire as ever entirely undesirable, since it is what drives the imagination. Rereading this book, I realize how often heaven, if it appears at all, appears as an earthly place, a place of change, of renovation and loss.

Even as I write this, there's a war escalating overseas and in my television. The horror is inescapable, as is the feeling that to escape horror altogether would constitute another form of horror. It's the kind of situation that characteristically puts art on the defensive and so resembles what you find in poems like "Kurt Weill," "Alban Berg," "Shostakovich," and others. The odd intimacy and distance between art and life is nowhere more conspicuous than in the realm of music, that art form which seems so powerful in its persuasive immediacy, and yet, being only loosely referential, so unspecific in effecting social change. The cycle of poems on composers offered me a means not only of exploring my affection for these people and their music, but also of putting art on the defensive, of looking at ways in which art and life impinge and fail to impinge on one another.

Naturally people are not identical with their aesthetic terms; nevertheless, those terms encourage an experience of ourselves as "out there," made precarious by the otherness of the world as mirror—or more precisely, as darkened window: half-mirror, half-window. In "Winter's Apprentice," heaven reflects earth, though not exactly. In "Planetarium," the child names the parents, or so they imagine. And though few of these poems are explicitly autobiographical, they are all implicitly so—often in ways I don't fully understand. Even more than music, it seems, words give us the sense of inhabiting a place that in turn inhabits us. They are the traces we leave in one another's rooms. It makes me feel indistinct, just thinking of it.

For all women, sung and unsung

" . . . the light stir
of the dust
that goes on dancing
long after the feet that raised it
have gone by."
                    Eleanor Wilner,
        "So Quietly the World" *Shekhinah*

GERALDINE C. LITTLE

Women: In the Mask and Beyond

GERALDINE LITTLE, born in Portstewart, Ireland, left it at the ag
of two. Her books include *Hakugai: Poem From a Concentratio.
Camp* (a book-length narrative poem on the incarceration c
Japanese-Americans during World War II); *A Well-Tuned Har*
Heloise & Abelard: A Verse Play (given its première performanc
at The Nicholas Roerich Museum, New York City, in March, 1990
and *Beyond the Boxwood Comb* (Six Women's Voices from Japan
Among her many awards. she has had a PEN Syndicated Sho
Fiction Award and grants in poetry and fiction from The New Jerse
Council on the Arts. She teaches at Burlington County Colleg
Currently she sings with The Choral Arts Society of Philadelphi
Her poem "Celebrations and Elegies for a Friend Dead of Aids"
being set to music by composer Jeffrey Bernstein.

CONTENTS

I. THE PRESENT TO ABOUT 1784

Vision 8
The Car 9
For Jacqueline du Pré, Cellist Extraordinaire 10
Keeping the Word: Chant Royal for Anna Akhmatova 11
Ravings from a Mental Institution: Ida Dalser 13
Elegy in Syllabics: Setsuku, wife of Balthus 17
Vignettes: Suzanne Valadon 19
Reminiscences: Victorious Life, Olive Schreiner 23
In the "House of Special Purpose," 26
Two Stalks in a Garden (Jane Wells and Rebecca West) 27
Vision: Mary Cassatt in Her Last Years 30
Paris Attic: Marya Sklodovska, Madame Curie 31
Suzuki: After Years—Considerations on the Child 33
Reflections: Mette-Sophie Gad (Mrs. Gauguin) 35
For Verdi's Retarded Sister, at their Father's Inn 36
Meditation: After Singing the Verdi Requiem 37
Marie d'Agoult: Three Songs 39
Crystalline Mind: Marchioness Ossoli, Margaret Fuller 41
Revelations: Rosa Bonheur 44
Mary Ludwig in Old Age 47
Wild Dreamer (Charlotte Corday) 49
Poem for Annette Vallon, French Mistress of Wordsworth 50
Phillis Wheatley: Soliloquy 52

II. 1600 A.D. TO ABOUT 751 A.D.

Soliloquy: Mrs. Magdalen Herbert 55
Madrigal for Margaret 56
Lines for Hwang Chin-I 56
Diptych: Harlinde and Renilde 58
The "Ada" School 59

III. BIBLICAL WOMEN—FIRST CENTURY A.D.

Mary of Magdala   61
Triptych: Three Mothers   63

IV. ABOUT 1200 B.C.

Aftermath (Ismene)   69
Abishag: Recollections in Old Age   73
Helen: The Dark Interior   75
One of the Suitors' Harlots   76

AFTERWORD   79

I. THE PRESENT TO ABOUT 1784

VISION

The dark is darker now, the woman curled
in fetal fashion on wide stone steps
mumbled as I stepped around her on my way
to sing in the great concert hall.

Inside swagged greenery cast shadows
in tall candles' light and rich red velvet bows
looped the lovely Christmas tale of love
come down for healing. Golden trumpets
fanfared against blustery cold.

Winter solstice now is ten days past.
Snowbirds write footsongs on snow.
Stars understand lesser darkened hours,
and threadlike roots, small bellpulls rung
as if by tiny wakened angels,
chime towards light

blurred by bones chattering a message
echoing in stone, like jungle drums
that warn and eerily wane.
I try to catch the words:

       hallowed?   holy?

but I've gone hollow, have sidestepped
too far from myths that promise miracle.

I remember that her eyes were green
and, childlike, gathered
what little light there was.

THE CAR

In Memoriam, Anne Sexton

Sure there were jolly times, jouncing to lunches
with literary pals, or picnics with kids all punches
and wisecracks (until you noticed their vulnerable eyes,
especially the daughters' reflecting their mother's).
    Memorialize
endings if you want but remember the lively lines
flung in a folder on my backseat under pines
after a workshop. What you don't know is they fired
my tired upholstery until I flamed, wired
to God, maybe, during one batch rowing
night's dark water. White sheets shivered, towing
their freight of need, rose up like offerings, I
the bewildered altar, blinded by the long cry,
each syllable a tear. Would I rust to ruin? I tell you
each trip was a journey; I often hated the view.
Back and forth to Bedlam I carried her, weighted
by all her burdened prettiness, she baited
by Death, his stuckout tongue, his chameleon-hide,
sweet as a lover's, in a second a snake's. Snide,
luring, clever, more steadfast than Life, that traitor
I watched play her false so often. Which was Creator,
which Killer? The question's creaked in my springs ever since

The moon sits in my emptiness. Sometimes I convince
myself she's coming to me, smiling, her gait
slightly whiskey-tilted. I listen. I wait.
But there is only the wind sighing its dirge
so like the one it sang when the awful urge
overwhelmed. Or was it Death whispering again
his promise: *Come, I'll keep you safe. Amen.*
What could a body, metal, brainless, do,
no matter its heart howled in the cold blue
afternoon for another chance, another ride
towards Parnassus? I cuddled her, choking, no pride

in my exhausted air that swirled like arms
unable to hold her, hold her back. Charms
sirened from another world always known, crooked
ringed tapered fingers beckoned. How eagerly she looked
into the beautiful terrible face. I heard
the bells she heard, the fairytales that stirred
but never satisfied. I saw her night,
her starry night and knew that was the light
she had to follow. I kept a single hair,
from it can conjure the whole woman bare
in her bones no matter what she wore. I gave
her what she wanted, a Saviour who could not save.

FOR JACQUELINE DUPRÉ, CELLIST EXTRAORDINAIRE
STRICKEN AT AN EARLY AGE WITH A FATAL ILLNESS

But some beauty is *not* momentary in the mind.
Perfected overtones in ether stay, and stars
after all midnights hold full shining. Do we forget
in sun true north? The poem, the poet dumb?

I think of how earth is glass, how all bear splinters,
soon or late, passports. This one, this one, this one
goes only jagged the whole journey, seeing always
in glass darkly. I think of how you mirrored Venus,
flashed that light back and forth, faultless message
on faultless glass before the creeping striae fractured.

Philosophy is facile. I would wish you Venus
rising eighty years and some, or eighty years
with lesser light, at least give choice. Small
as a white flower I once gathered on a moor,
no god deploying genes, I only can remember
the fine web spun on the flower, the way a wind.
bowed crisp concerti on those strings, full
on the fall of thirty years as in that moment's music.

10 LITTLE

KEEPING THE WORD: CHANT ROYAL

> *What though the dead be crowded, each to each,*
> *What though our houses be destroyed?*
> *We will preserve you, Russian speech,*
> *Keep you alive, great Russian word.*
>
> *And so nothing in the world*
> *is stronger than I,*
> *And I can bear anything, even this.*
> Anna Akhmatova

Oil lamp. A curve of yellow burns night
on the Black Sea Coast where you bloom into day
of your first breath. Mirrors hold the light
in walnut frames, give back light to play
on rustling skirts, plush chairs, a density
of old plaid rugs, a samovar, tea
steaming towards June crickets. You would confide
"the patterned silence" of your childhood, slide
the hurt into smoothest words, versing
how the voice of wind could override
lack, speaking to your understanding.

Christmas, 1903. Streets a white
whirl, you meet your fate on the way
to buy tree baubles: Gumilyov, polite
and smitten by your too-pale face, grey
wild bird eyes. He saw in you the sea,
you *in* sea, water nymph in filigree
of foam and deeper currents, saw his bride-
to-be, bride only after suicide
attempts, two, his florid frenzied offering
to love's burning, singed. You denied
misgivings, wed, flew to Paris. Spring

is always Paris, always poetry. Right
bank and left trembled under sway
of giants seized by Muses. Erudite,
innocent, sometimes dark as death, they
touched the tongue of Mandelstam, esprit
of you, to song, dirge, singularity
of words. Gumilyov named you witch. Not soft-eyed
son could stitch the jagged deep divide
that marriage was, and so the others. A thing
all wing and fire, how could you abide
the bars of ordinary, pinions beating?

And Mandelstam whispered *Cassandra*. Death your sight.
Or vision? War and revolution must slay
old orders. In dark mists of new, might
hammered hell on spines of all. *Obey
or die*: they died, not always dead. Not free,
a state more stifling than earthtomb where tree
is root, and worms give back a hard-held pride
in leaf, flower and fruit. All too clear-eyed,
could you think of flowers, every morning
heavy with news: arrest, at eventide
a death of someone who once shared your singing?

"Half harlot and half nun." Human. Bright
edging blight, the common lot, but protegée
of Parnassian gods, you were sprite
strung on steel. Shall we speak of flay-
ing cold, hand of leaching poverty
that served black bread, tea rarely,
and sugarless, the trek to queue beside
a sleeted prison wall, hoping to slide
a parcel to a son blue-lipped, thinning
there an eon of fourteen years? How ride
winds of crushing weather? Such a suffering

moved you to the Cross, the bereft Mary
under stars of death gleaming coldly.
Ruin to Requiem. Dignified
in loss of all, you stand, luminous guide
to lived endurance in poems that throb like praying.
And boats go quietly down the Neva, glide
through willows touched autumnal, all stars burning.

RAVINGS FROM A MENTAL INSTITUTION: IDA DALSER

I.
Scribblings.
Harmless.
What can an old woman, in tatters,
shadows of her snarled white hair
like worms on the water-stained wall,
dark skin dirt-streaked,
babbling,
do to anyone?
Disbelief is the bird
shadowing scraps of paper
and the half-finger-length pencil
they let me have.

What year is this? 1920? 35? 36?
Who can tell one day, one month, one year
from another?
Just a slit of light, like a dagger
they dangle to tease. No way
to seize it for stilling
my heart that crazily goes on
beating against bars
as if someone could hear.

Stupid old woman
to move over memories as fingers
moved over beads of the rosary
I told when I was a child,
before stones became cold, dark cobbles
like these I lie on,
stench of my own waste
the only incense.

II.

Editor of Avanti,
he boasts, chest testing seams
of his uniform.
We're draped under the arch of an arcade
in Milano (when? yesterday? forty years ago?),
my slit-black skirt leading him in
to the moon of me, the real moon
tumbling through cypresses.

Buono, Buono, I dimple,
not caring for anything
but the animal flare
of him over me I imagine
will be like God come
to His bride.

I'm young as a new grape,
as juicy.

Soon we stumble to the lake;
he's pressing me on the dark bank
as trees loose shadows
into silvery waters.
God's own rod, I whisper,
drunk on the drama of him.
Night birds blur.
But their songs are pure
music.

III.
What matter he's married to Rachele?
He lives with *me*,
promises marriage.
My hands like feathers light
on the round ball of my womb, big
with his baby.
Benito, I croon,
like you, a panther.

He beams, centers his cheek
on my bare belly,
almost bursts as the baby kicks.

A panther. His hands move
to my dark fur. Large as I am
we mesh, twist. Outside the window
a star skitters towards earth.
Lucky.
I make a wish.

IV.
Offices of Il Popolo
don't frighten me.
Here is your son, I shout
shoving towards him the skinny boy
with enormous head he made
in the hot nest of me
I scream, pace, threaten:
No maintenance money. MARRIAGE.
As you promised.
Anyway, I spit, *no money*
ever came.

Guards gag me, slap us both
half senseless, toss us
to darkness no straight pines mark

like points on a map.
Nothing to follow.
No way to go.
Hands, pockets empty
as withered pods.
Only this crippled seed-child beside me
rattling in hostile winds.

V.

What does a woman have
who has nothing
but her voice? I raise it
in cafes and conferences, again, again.
Always his black henchmen handle me
and Benito like sticks of wood
they pile on a pyre.
I flame. They burn
us to nothing.

VI.

To shut me up
he forcibly confined me
here. How long ago?
I used to try to scratch sunrises
on the wall with a hairpin.
They took all hairpins: dangerous.
To what? Who?

I am a lunatic. Am I?
My mind *does* wander
down strange alleys, pinched streets.
Where is the boy, Benito?
When was it they took him?
Was he real or did I dream him
flying out of me, an angel
made by God?

Is that him in the corner,
eyes red as lamps
that used to wink *love*
on Milano streets?

Benito, Benito.
I grope towards the figure.
It bites me.
A rat.
I no longer shudder.
It sprints away dragging the dream.
The way of rats.

I embrace the dwarf-size pencil.
What does a destitute woman have
but her voice?

ELEGY IN SYLLABICS: SETSUKU, WIFE
OF THE FRENCH-POLISH PAINTER BALTHUS

The cry of plovers
wakes me from the uneasy
dream to the nightmare.

How dark it is. Stars
banished, in the black sky the
blacker round I seem

to see, the moon's dead
socket. Sleep has whined into
that waste. No wild birds

beat on the glass of
my husband's rest. His breath rides
a gentler tide, like

my baby's. Oh. I
dam the wound of sobs in my
mouth with cool covers.

When my bereft bones
stop rocking, I slide away
to his easel, white,

blank as my womb. Child,
how will he draw you, you dead
in your vase of worms?

Sweet firstborn, will he
remember the willow bud
of you at my breast?

What brush will trace the
light tricks of your eyes shadowed
by butterflies? What

pigment will fix your
breath silken as petals un-
furling? Still crying,

plovers, you fade, faint
on wind rasping to dawn. What
sun can lighten loss?

VIGNETTES: SUZANNE VALADON

1.

At the Place Pigalle Fountain
before the eyes of artists, sizing-up,
we parade, turn, slouch,
haggle for rates, pose
till last light,
at dusk move into a fizz
of chatter at the brasserie
on the boulevard. *Green absinthe.*
Food that burns.

Whoever has money pays.

I tilt to a cabaret, float
to bed with any partner, come
back to the world, wild
birds beating. But I can't think
of birds. The crush at the fountain,
the elbowing for jobs, the hunger
for coins....
I spin to the fountain.

2.

Here, everyone paints.
Art's my constant, lover
with lines I can fondle,
shape to *my* ends.

After the work, the perspective
of a cafe: Catalan dances:
contrepas, sardanas.
The man Utrillo shakes
le Chat Noir with deft steps.
Shakes *me*, twirls
in my body, more frantic

than most.
Strange how a monthly absence
of blood can bloom
to a bulge in the belly.
Is it Miguel Utrillo's?
Puvis de Chavannes'?
I laugh while gossips guess.
Utrillo feeds me money;
who needs a name?

3.
The day after Christmas
fir-scent is all
red scream. A son
kicks air.

Maurice: Not to suckle.

He must learn my breasts
are our bread.

4.
Charigot so charming—
a bitch! After she beats me
out of Renoir's bed
and board, I find
wood violets at the bottom
of Lautrec's eyes.

Little Lautrec, large
wound of himself open
to my purse of troubles.

I tell him as I tell you:

"Maurice has seizures.
Grand'mere Madeleine

quiets him with chabrot.
The next day another
explosion."

He listens exquisitely,
squints at my work —

"Come, we'll show this
to Degas."

I forget, almost,
Maurice's tempests.

5.

"In his moments at home,
teach him how to paint."

The doctor's chancy prescription
for Maumau, my Maurice. I teach him
line, color, the wash of the world
on a small white space.

He paints walls, walls, walls.
You want to touch the torn
leeching urine stains,
want to walk down his streets
away from the stinking world
he ranges, mumbling
in winemist.

6.

Out of a sky littered
with clouds, I find
Andre Utter. Utter,
able to bear even Maumau.
We manage a menage à trois
in Montmartre. Utter's young

arms dance hard
round my creaking flesh.

*But Maumau reels
to the black country.*

7.
Bugles, bugles, bugles:
War jangles Montmartre
that loves parties.
This one's gayer, larger,
a costume ball.

Utter marches off.
We marry first. No solace.

8.
In the middle of Armistice
revelry, cool in that din,
we mount an exhibition:

VALADON-UTRILLO-UTTER

How I wanted Utter,
back from war, amorous
and eager, to sell.
He sells nothing,
turns sly, ferrets
for canvases covering
Montmartre:
Maurice's, paid out for drinks
down every hellish street.

I become rich!
I think: golden shoes,
pomegranates, peregrines...

Maurice smashes his head
against the gendarmes' wall
O my mad Mauma.

... and know the world
is dirty bones.

9.
Brush poised over a bowl
of flowers, I move
back: my mother's beatings,
school, nuns prodding me
read, write. Move
beyond walls, Maumau.

Light
explodes.

REMINISCENCES:
VICTORIOUS LIFE, OLIVE SCHREINER

1.
My father had little formal learning
but great knowledge of God, a simple man
called to his mission in South Africa

out of the plain food of German
peasantry. He taught me how the heart
must be wide as the world, how loving

is the song everyone needs. My mother
moved on her fine English bones from the Lake
District, all watery light and birdsong.

In middle life I married an Englishman
but I thought and think of myself as a child
of the Great Karoo, that shelf so like the sea,

always, yet never, the same, full of laughter,
cruel, coldly inhuman, beautiful under fierce suns,
frozen stars, land of passionate extremes.

Like Charlotte Bronte, at twenty I flew out
of the nest into the world as governess
for a Karoo farmer. Even in a primitive land

my quarters were primeval. I slept, lived, wrote
in a miniscule mud-floored outhouse. I tried
to be steely, to remember my father's faith
        about loving,

but the boisterous, headlong children... I left
for a better post, still in the Karoo, where
all spoke Afrikaans. There was a pinch of comfort,

no less loneliness. Before it was fashionable I talked
to small succulent plants struggling for life
near stones on the dry plain. I meditated

beside a clump of prickly pears lifting thorny arms
towards the moon reflected in broad fleshy leaves.
I wandered sheep kraals, Kaffir huts

in search of myself, slipped into an ostrich camp
and down a plume to safe darkness before
wrestling back to the moon-flushed desk

where I scribbled to murder black seizures
of asthma rattling one rib against another, multiple
hands on my throat stricturing speech, stealing air,

devils out of my father's Book.
Is it stifling makes us form other worlds?
Out of what gasping dream did Lyndall and Waldo

move across the plain of my life like the flowered
loveliness of "bloom-tyd," springing my spirit,
revealing raw unwithering roots?

2.

You imagine after the hard writing
my *African Farm* stepped into print easily
as a lamb drops from its mother's womb.

You imagine I flew to England on Fame's
realized wings. Listen, the manuscript spun
round publishing houses until I was dizzy, battered

ill by vultures of rejection. Listen,
I had to take the name "Ralph Iron" to sell
the length of cloth woven in the shadow

of milk trees cutting out sky. By accident,
out of my choking need, I tumbled from my time
into yours when women's voices sing out

of darkness, vibrant, strong, when in my continent
links of long chains break in necessary angers,
littering the land I sprung from, I

understanding the free life is the life
that must be lived. It is well "to see darkness
breaking and the day coming...to see

the new time breaking..." The dream rises
from thorn-pod to flower, and strongly holds
light, leaf after leaf after leaf, light

above bloodied veldt and Karoo, the kicked bones
of becoming all that is written in the seed's code,
the fulfillment, the important greening.

IN THE "HOUSE OF SPECIAL PURPOSE,"
EKATERINBURG, MAY, 1918: ANASTASIA

> *"Anastasia was a charming little devil, such a bag of*
> *mischief that no one could ever be bored in her*
> *company. Lively and always on the move, she was*
> *continually pulling funny faces... as they do in the*
> *circus."*
> —Eugen Platonovitch N.

Light's on the low hills. I know, though night
is our constant time. Stupid to let myself dream
tea and black bread will *not* be our breakfast. *May*
and the lilacs are budding Tsarkoe Selo. Time
for prayers, Papa calls. Quietly. Still, the guard
follows me to the lavatory. I blush. And hate.

Why do we pray, and to whom? How He must hate
us. *Oh!* I rinse my mouth of the dark night
of such sin. Olga's eyes are closed. The guard
leers at the door. I sway in the murmuring dream.
I am riding my pony on the curved track times
changed cannot steal, in the green brilliance of May.

Yes. Tea and black bread. But later we may
walk in the garden! However much we hate
alien eyes always on us, there is that time
of light and birds to hold against the night
we wear like dirty clothes in a villain's dream.
In the garden even Mama drops her guard

a moment until her eyes lift to the guard's.
Then the Tsaritsa appears and the small patch of May
withers to winter. Where has she gone? Does she dream
of the mauve room she loved? Does evident hate
mask her drifting away to jewelled nights
in the palace, balalaikas keeping her loveliest time?

Behind my eyes, less cool than Mama's, time
takes me to my own kind of winter. Nothing that guard,
fouleyed and mouthed, can image. After crystalline night,
crystalline mornings. *Papa, dear Papa, may
we make ice mounds?* So we toboggan, hating,
loving the wind's cold slaps. Oh I could dream

down these days till I'm lost in my moans, dream,
dragging all with me. So I laugh, time
my queer faces for when theirs are saddest, hate
reined taut in every jokeline.... That one guard,
is his glint of compassion a mockery? Just May
madness coloring my sight, scenting the night,

night when I dream again. My spaniel runs
in another May, keeping time at my heels.
Beside me now, his breath guards, stanches hate.

TWO STALKS IN A GARDEN

1.   Amy Catherine Robbins Wells (Jane)

White and purple Michaelmas daisies. I loved
them always, at once passionate and prim. I arrange
their glory crowning a crystal bowl, place
them on a polished table that gathers their shadows,
those undersides so rarely seen. Sunlight
warms his absence. The room is full. And still.

Full of will. Mine, that daily stills
sooty birds' scratching. Why do I love
a man who hurts me again and again, lightly,
insouciantly as a bee stings, his arrangements
with others barely concealed? Is it the shadow
of long ago guilt, myself in the murky place

of mistress, little thought given to Isabel's place,
cousin-wife he discarded for me? I still
remember the thrill of his torrented speech over-
shadowing sense and morals. *That* was what I most
loved, love now. His flashing tongue can never arrange
itself to shape dull syllables. He *is* light

for me, as I am, I believe, the steady light
of his life. "Moral governess," my place,
someone said, "Jane," who always arranges
perfectly home, garden, society's still
expectant (and gossipy) demands, no matter what love
he lies with wrapped in the moon's illusory shadows.

How splendid the great oaks, their tangled shadows
this morning, after rain, painted with light,
path through them a pattern of wings and lovely
song. Oh, Easton Glebe: place
of refuge, place where I draw myself up to still
grandeur, in its weave of gardens work to arrange

bones of a life to flesh, despite his arrangements
elsewhere, he loves to fondle. I am *not* his shadow,
not "Jane." I am Catherine, writing my still
stories, landscapes touched with evening light,
Catherine, scented with serenity, the only place
he comes home to, my brilliant, damaged, little-boy love.

Lovely, lovely, the daisies, random arrangement
my place, my part, the bee unaware of its shadow.
So light, and, after all, winged. Still.

2.Cicely Fairfield (Rebecca West)

A profusion of Michaelmas daisies the first time
I went to lunch at Easton Glebe: strong
colors somehow quietly in control
of the room. The definition of Jane, I later
learned, clever wife who kept him by loosest
reins and perfected peace. His arrogant mind

was a magnet. I'd massacred his *Marriage* in print. He minded
sufficiently to notice me, 22, time
racing towards waste, I thought, eager to loose
myself, my ideas on literary London strongly
ruled by men missing the essence of latest
thinking by women on women. Beyond their control

was SHE who was not a Pygmalion. I spoke of control
(vivaciously, he said later). Jane didn't mind,
didn't agree or disagree. A lady. *Lately*
we've been bothered with mites. Have you time
to walk round the gardens? I remember immense strong
hollyhocks, a drift of late dahlia-scent loose

on September air. How easily a woman loses
herself in autumn's seductive thrust controlled
by the year's speeded ticking.... We lie in strong
morning light in a picturesque place, minds
forgotten, wet with each other, wheeling timely
tufts of birdsong trembling in. Later

we walk the Amalfi coast, picnic in late
afternoon on chicken, wine by the sea loose
in its net of clouds and gull shadows. When does time
sweet in a lover's arms turn bitter, controlled
by untamable forces no matter how bright the mind,
how sure the talent? Listen, I loved the strong

child that was ours, child who knew me as strong
"Aunty Panther," loved Wells later
than sense dictated. I know that a woman's mind
is her only malleable refuge. I gathered the loose
scattered remnants of mine, determined to control
my life, grave my name on the stones of time.

What will time make of us, three stalks strong
in a corner of England? Beyond control, late
daisies loose in the wind sway on the mind.

VISION: MARY CASSATT IN HER LAST YEARS

The pond at Beaufresne in early summer holds
the flash of trout turning, turning in sunlight
rain will shortly blur, softly, only
a suggestion of clouds idling across blue sky.

Strawberries in the garden flesh towards bright
perfection, asparagus elegantly slim will nudge
palates to quiet delirium. Magnificent trees
burgeon: buds, birdtalk, a weave of nests.

In the oval dining room a woman sits
erect and weathered under the mirrored ceiling
reflecting lamps, candles lit for luncheon:
fresh trout, salad, a fine Chateau Margot.

After Mathilde clears, Mary moves
to the garden. The rain has passed, making luminous
petals, stalks, slugs diligently nibbling.
She sits on an old bench in the washed air.

Now she lives in the dark world of her blindness.
What good to speak of irony, of how fate
and time can steal essential senses, blacken
brightest vision? Bitterness is not a color

permitted in her palette or on the canvas
stretched behind the traitorous eyes. The white
space is alive, vigorous with passionate belief
in the importance of art, revelations of life

lived whatever the terms. At her desk she writes,
almost illegibly, "I take a great interest in keeping
all going. It is much to have an object in life."
She pauses to sniff white and garnet roses,

her loved roses of Beaufresne fragrant
on air filling an open window. How clearly
she sees their shadows delicate on yielding soil,
feels, understands, the inevitable prick of thorns

as Mathilde places a bouquet in her hands
moved always by intricately innocent impressions
of her life, the rich pastels and subtleties of France,
the staid resonances of Philadelphia.

PARIS ATTIC: MARYA SKLODOVSKA, MADAME CURIE

> "It is your destiny so to move your wand,
> To wake up storms, to run through the heart of storms."
> — from "Day of Generation," Czeslaw Milosz

You understand I loved him, Casimir, witty,
animated. Didn't he bustle me out to hear
the threadbare young Pole, face framed by coppery hair,
woo the piano to birdlilt and thunder, Paderewski?
Didn't he, evenings at home, charm us to laughter?

But I couldn't stopper ears against night calls
of his patients, couldn't shut out footsteps of messengers
who came for Bronya to help with a wife's confinement.

The threads of a difficult equation spiralled away
in that jangle of sound, concentration lost, and temper!

So I moved here, this cell of solitude: a loophole
of light slants in from the roof, no water, no heat.
But see how this is home. Mattress from Poland,
stewpan, white wooden table, kitchen chair,
washbasin (which holds bright shadows of birds!),
saucer-sized heater for cooking...
                              and I can walk to school.
In all weather the Sorbonne stands, stern haven
of my every hope. What matter I feed on berries,
tea, quick swallows of air. I live by light
in the lab. And just beyond winter, lilacs, fruit-trees.

*

July. The examiner enters, prepares to read
names of the elect in order of merit: First,
            Marie Sklodovska
A beat of wild birds at the heart's revealed windows.
"The chestnuts are blooming.... Everything is green."*
(*portion of a letter from Marie to those at home in Poland.)

SUZUKI: AFTER YEARS
—CONSIDERATIONS ON THE CHILD

"Here's more, dear Mistress."
"It is not enough yet."
—*"Flower Duet," Madame Butterfly, Puccini*

Here, mist is always plum-scented

This country is mountainous. Snow
glosses slanted masses long,
long into foothills of summer.
Odd lichens bury their shadows
in longer, still breathing. My choice
was hard living: opium
of scratching for sticks, in stands
of slick white bears, for fires,
hanging my hut from a hillside
after gouging its bones out of stumps
resistant as robbers caught.

Steeped rose leaves: tart pungent tea

On a table, bruise-colored iceplant
in a crock I formed, firing
spring-released clay. Stalks shade
his letter. *She* taught me
the revelations of characters
I mastered, she content
with sketchy outlines, a bird
gilded simply for taking
eyes. Through the years
I have not answered missives
he cries from a colder land.

Camelias: the brown of their fading

Yenless, homeless, a mite
in their minds, I could not keep him.
The cuts of his small fists scarred
my bones gone slack in the slime
of her silence. I was crippled
in cleaning her littered love.
What could I write him? "Love
is a myth you must never read"?
"She was foolish to think he took fragrance
for earth-planted seeds of perennials."?
Bitter berries numbed tongue and hands.

Cherry limbs, gnarled and frost-killed

Faltering now, he is
resigned, no longer rebellious,
no longer a poor wild thing
trapped in a frozen forest,
writhing, wailing, trying
to bite itself free, drowning
in pooling blood he sees
too clearly his own. A father's
terrible presents, a wife's
airy annoyance: "half-caste
in any land. You were careless."

Verbena's too sweet in the spring

I will burn them, some winter, kindling
not found, and carefully shovel
out ash. Winds will reply
from the dead-letter days of my dying.

REFLECTIONS: METTE-SOPHIE GAD
(Mrs. Gauguin)

Can I eat them, canvases
I trip over, maimed
by awkward angles?

What use was he anyway, dead
in the night to my blood's hungers,
live by day only
to *his* blood's thrust
to putter among paint-pots?

I look at five mouths spread
for some kind of feeding,
choke on the bile of love's
reality he fled.

It was trompe l'oeil, the painting
presented, unstable wash
I thought durable, strong
in any light. Bleeding,
I see another canvas, mauve
lakes, exuberant farms, beaches,
windmills by drafty castles,
in the chimneys of home, storks
folding into roosts
like pocketed charms. I hear

the silken kiss of the Skaggerak,
the Tivoli's tunes.

Oh to be wash,
able to run off in rivers
exposing a virgin canvas.
But I was always oil,
deep-layered, made
to last.

How did we come
to mix media? I shiver
at five reflections
half water, half oil.

FOR VERDI'S RETARDED SISTER, AT THEIR FATHER'S INN

                    Innocence
is its own miracle,
the one dropped petal
ringing ever wider
ripples, like a brother's sounds
circling, circling her stream
of consciousness, coloring the black
apron she wears standing in sunlight
filling the kitchen doorway, wild
garlic pungent in undemanding
                            hands.

MEDITATION:
AFTER SINGING THE VERDI REQUIEM

—for Guiseppina Strepponi

After the momentary hush, the applause,
the sparks challenging stars, I went away
to walk beside a creek in a wooded park.
Mid-afternoon; it had been a morning
performance, memoriam for a famous man.

A flat rock, sunlit, alive with shadows
of birds, trees, and one great fern's fronds.
I sat on it, my stirred thoughts ran
like a current in the water, not to Verdi,
irrefutable genius, but to you
in your last moments apologizing to him:
ill with pneumonia you could not smell the flower
he brought you, senses and light beginning to dim.

Opera star. Stages strewn with flowers.
How little we know of the petal's underside.
You were rented out by an agent to any
impressario, without your approval, pride
pocketed for what you needed most: money,
you sole support of a widowed, illiterate
mother, younger siblings, your own child,
illegitimate, lost in history's footnotes.

Four or five times a week you sang, hours
of strain that ripped your voice almost beyond
repair, some married lover—who?—a bee
sucking honey, offering no substance, flying
at dusk back to his hive. Your letters speak
of suicidal thoughts, withdrawal. A crying
flails the sunsplashed rock as if to crack it.

Seasons change. After witherings, awakenings.
Verdi dedicated *Jerusalem* to you
busy now with pupils. In summer's healing
light, together you rented a house in Passy,
with a garden: flowers, always flowers, theme
in the undulating opus of your life.

Verdi is busy with the grotto and the garden,
you wrote...*happier believing nothing,*
but you, devout, wanted the marriage of rose
with strong stem, wanted legitimacy.
Thorns rip even the silkiest salons of repose.

What brought him to union in 1859, who knows,
motivations elusive as clouds that, reforming, pass
from view. Threats of war? His decision to stand
as a public official? One understands (not crass)
the benefits: you could inherit as *real* widow.
No matter he grumbled, found fault whatever you did—
some days. Genius has its own unfecund plots.

The yellowing, the browning of petals, the turning years.
In Montecatini, he 83, you 81,
bent with arthritis, still, as a friend wrote,
offering "a suggestion of old beauty,"
he must have seen, bending, at the end, to kiss
your dead chilled cheek, his flushed, no tears,
then standing motionless beside a barren table.

No funeral flowers, crowds, or speeches, you said,
and so it was, and so I compose these reflections
for you, on a rock dusk chills, a Requiem
of Roses, fragrant, hardy, for you, unsung.

MARIE D'AGOULT: THREE SONGS

I. In Italy
How tenderly rough the nap of your jacket I lean
against, Liszt, in a sudden wind from the sea.
Above us, gulls curve patterns of praise never seen
before by any lovers. Shells perpetually
shifting make unique song: everything new
in this Italian air we share by day
and by passionate night after night when you
whirl on the moon of me and together we play
at nothing composed by mortals. Brilliantly wild,
weeds we romp through on a nearby hill.
I tickle your chin with a buttercup, laugh at your mild
annoyance, soon erased by my wiles and will.
Liszt, I've made a wish on the innocent flower:
May we live forever, together, in love's lucent bower.

II. In Paris
Everyone's left my salon. I push at taut
face muscles, mask formed by ceaseless smiling.
Franz, these receptions now are famous. You ought
to come to Paris instead of stubbornly whiling
away your time on tour. You like brilliant talk;
it is here: Lamartine, Victor Hugo, Gautier vie
endlessly. Enchanting! Like nimble-eyed hawks
they swoop on silence as if to mice. We sigh,
simper, gossip, flirt before mirrors rimmed
in gold, our breath moving tall candles' light
to intriguing shapes. Oh we are never dimmed,
my dear. Your metier. Everything bright
on the Faubourg St. Honoré. *Except it is raining
and I dare not write you how dismal my desperate feigning.*

III. In Paris, Another Mode, Later

What can I dangle to entice? Certainly not
our illegitimate children now in your mother's
keeping. Although you owned entirely my hot
responsive flesh, *mother*, not *mistress*, smothers
love's thrust every time. For you. You address me now
as Madame, forgetting Marie, that girl once on flame
at your fingers' touch. As everyone is. I vow
I won't write, but here I am, playing your game
again, chagrined that I manage minor keys only
though you want to hear all in major: Montez's keys,
everyone says. *Tinny*, I shriek, lonely
to lunacy's edge. Ranting. Jealous. Diseased.
But I've written our dream of love, sweet love. You'll hear
of my novel *Nelida*. You with your perfect ear.

CRYSTALLINE MIND:
MARCHIONESS OSSOLI, MARGARET FULLER

I. Cambridge, Ma. May 23, 1810
Cattails and maples evidence knowledge
of light. Air: assemblage of scents.

In a crock wild grasses gathered at dawn
sweeten a woman's room. Someone
is singing. The lullaby hangs in the window
a night's endurance of labor swirls
through, dark scenes exchanged for May's
exuberances, fresh life. Margaret
is golden, Margaret sips with soft
pussy willow lips. Margaret, Margaret,
shape with those lips "lux eterna,"
imbibe nurturing Grecian syntax.

Hurry, Margaret, hurry. May
tilts tornado-like towards endings.

II. Cambridge, Later
stress of strophes
imprinted by rote

        the reel of stick and rod
amo, amas
stuffed into cells

        the sway and dip of books
spectral illusions,
nightmares, sleepwalking

        the dance becoming dirge
habits formed
flare to passion

        the light steps of languages learned

III. Journey
After you see your father stern with rigor
mortis, holding class in his coffin, after

flowers fold on stone, you pack your tongues,
body of books, vigorous veins of learning
off to Boston and Bronson Alcott's visions.

But your visions are your own, transcending
common conceptions. How your conversation
classes for women slit clouds, exposing star-
light possibilities for growth. *Fair
chance for females*, the innovative creed you cherish
in your book, shoots it to unexplored galaxies:
Women of the Nineteenth Century: read   soar

IV. Moving On
English panorama   French ambience
but Italy, Italy moves into your bones
    like marrow. Through your senses spin
        Petrarch, Pirandello, Verdi,
           flowers of Florence
              grapes   pasta   olives
shine like Venetian glass
clear as your crystalline mind.
Love is your personal Renaissance,
marriage your incomparable city.
Rome besieged by revolution:
    you halo a hospital,
    take charge like a benevolent priestess
    brilliantly easing
        maimed, the poor, the dying
    while your husband fights
    on the walls, a Roman warrior

V. Joy
Another labor: issue
    a son, perfect
    as Jesu bambino
to you hearing
    grasses croon

flowers sing
birds whoop

VI. The Snuffed Flame

Another May: fields fruited, full
        of the miracle: sun
You move with your miracle
        son and husband towards
        America, waves
           doubling, tripling until June
           with its flowing tides
           sees you just off
shore, waves moving like avalanches
        foaming, spinning
               wrecking
forever
        your vessel's timbers
        on the beaches of Fire Island

VII. Questions

Margaret, walking the sea's fathoms,
        are your footsteps light on sea grasses?
Is the baby, the son
        in your arms, laughing at toys,
        the twisting tentacles?
Does he move beside you,
        the man, the husband, sharing
        your restless questioning
        of that spectacular world?

Daisies rise wild beyond the dunes,
a gull settles into its shadow moaning

    Margaret, forty was too young
    for death
    for the burning out
    in that cold fire

REVELATIONS: ROSA BONHEUR

1. *First Visit to the Horse Market, Boulevard*
   de l'Hôpital Near the Asylum of la Salpêtrière

The trees, in full leaf, hide me, until I corner
sufficient courage to think of moving in
to that plunging, raucous blur of men and horses
pounding, rearing on dusty cobbles. What a din!

Even dressed as I am, like a man, will they
accept me, that rowdy jumble of traders? How
long I looked for pants just baggy enough
to camouflage curving hips, a shirt so the sway

of breasts wouldn't be noticed, scrounged a frock coat,
decided against it—a bit too much for *this*
brawl of flesh. My cap's the crowning note,
snares my hair, gives me an impudent look,

I think, like some of those boys pulling at bridles,
tugging at reins, arms, hands strongly
muscled, skin moving over bones I can see
come alive on my sketch pad now, now as I watch.

Oh the pull of the Percherons! Breasts like these
bore knights in full armor. They rise before me, kingly
in battle under their clanking masters. One
massive grey/white horse snorts near. I seize

aura of his passionate breath, furiously work
to capture, quickly, his flanks, structure beneath
before he swirls back to the pack. On the hoof-marked heath
green shirts, blue shirts flash. I brush in sky

they're blind to, wind-pushed white over the sweating
teeming turbulence. I must get closer to the thing,

feel part of the heated scene, the cursing, the swopping.
Nerves ticking, I gulp, swagger into the mêlée.

2. *After the Salon of 1853:*
    In the Pyrenées with Nathalie Micus

The wildness here suits me. After the heady
acclaim of my Horse Fair (Delacroix himself generous
beyond his wont, beyond *my* expectations),
the subtle, but sure, back-stabbings and gossip, steady

oaks, implacable firs and pines calm.
Not that it wasn't agreeable—as fame is—
though it has inconveniences. I thought I'd succeeded
in keeping my incognito here, but this

morning I received a downpour of cards from all quarters.
Since, our landlord (so proud, he says, to have me
in his house), has walked about the streets singing
my praises! Nathalie and I escaped to free

mountainous air. We spent a luminous day,
I sketching whatever wildlife dared
our strangeness: birds, squirrels at skittering play,
hare with ample haunches, Nathalie outlining

ideas for extraordinary inventions. I smoked
just one cigarette, after our picnic of wine,
chicken, impossibly light petit fours, not needing
their kick in that clear air. Sun poked

through chinks in the dark still foliage, peace
stroked our souls, and, Nathalie, dearest
love, we stroked each other's limbs and hearts
in that perfected state I hope may cease

never, we who know each other's stupidities,
mortifications, *and* triumphs, as no one

else. How you buoyed, endeavored to ease
pain of a plethora of rejection before the Salon

success. How you bear with my menagerie:
stench, feathers, fur, bellowings, barkings,
neighings, mewings, even doctoring them,
for, I am sure, only my sake...Daringly,

I made a date for tomorrow with Mariano,
famous smuggler whom no one can capture, who'll sit
for his portrait. A coup! He appears to have taken a fancy
to me, goes about with his shaggy brows knit

saying he'd give his life for me! Nathalie and I
(in our room) laugh, tenderly, for he's charming,
and who doesn't need admiration? Perhaps I can get
a few Havana cigars for Isidore. *Fie*

his frowning face said when I got my "Permission
de Travestissement" from the police allowing
me to wear male attire in public. Fie,
Isidore, for not understanding: comfort's the thing

with art and animals, for not understanding more
than I deign to discuss. Bulls I paint are the only
males I like, but I'll bring you a smuggler's smokes
for love's odd sake, brother I sometimes adore.

High over mountains, now, the full moon
reveals Chinese legend: a hare promising
elixir of immortality. Have I sipped it?
No matter. The work itself's the purest spring.

MARY LUDWIG IN OLD AGE

(Whom history knows as Molly Pitcher)

Once a year, like returning leaves, they come,
forty green dollars from the Government. My hands,
no longer steady, clutch them: food, heat,

light for the small world of my room. I pay
them out slowly, slowly. A jay shrieks at the windows,
raucous, brilliant. *Why do you hoard*, I believe

he scolds. *At your age, be warm, eat well.* He doesn't
yet know how age devours courage and heaven
is a country I can't believe though I want to, have

always wanted to. Look, if you've seen war,
seen boys spill on the land like a legacy
for worms, you want to believe they've gone to God.

Nights, sometimes, I take a tot of whiskey,
neat. (Oh, never mind pointing the finger,
you in your warm mantle of youth.) Before

my scant fire the mind plays tricks with time. I
am as young as you, just married. I see
the beautiful arc of his body over me, hear

lovewords no lady should know, that I *loved*. We
whir to an island dotted with birds: maroon,
jade, cream. They sing us to the only heaven

I *know* exists. Then we all explode, he,
I, birds, island, in an iridescent
flash. We sleep. Everything's right in our world.

Hell. I believe in *that*. At Monmouth, the heat
sucked wits and marrow. What was it all *about*,
anyway? Revolution? *Was anything worth the dying?*

Maggots in boyish flesh move through my dreams
still. And blood, carpeting greeny June
too richly. Johnny, Johnny, I screeched when he fell,

and sprang to his gun. Without thinking. Burning. Furious.
For Johnny. I began to understand something
of how war invades bones like a madness. My hands

on the gun. God! It was power, kicking, whining, flaming.
Beyond anything known. Yes, I ferried pitchers
of water, heart cracking at how those boys panted,

sweat rushing down blackened limbs. Yes.
I did that, couldn't do enough. But the gun.
In my hands...I aimed to kill. And make no apology

for it. A demon took over my body. War
at the moment excites while it damns. (*That's* the hell).
After, you weep in the gardens of bones, weep

that you could have planted some of them there (what matter
what side, what color the uniform), weep for what
you'd become...Then it was over. But it is never

over. My mind like a sleeping monster wakes up
when I most want peace, I, an old woman watching
leaves come and go, faster, faster each year,

who would like to think only of how it was when he came
to me first in the high hard bed, how his hand
round a cup of tea in the kitchen was tawny, and kind.

WILD DREAMER
MARIE ANNE CHARLOTTE CORDAY D'ARMONT
(1768-1793)

It was always a matter of vision. The country-
side of Caen, its haymows and wildflowers, the still
ordered mosaic of the convent stayed
like a chanting at dusk, lighting lonely
hours at Aunt's, obligato to books devoured, days
of my dreaming. First images last.

Excitement in Normandy at last!
The drowsy country
place, its simple days
roused for refuge! Still
speaking their downfalling, their lonely
cause, Girondin leaders stayed

in our calm air, the staid
round of rural. Last
(on purpose) at one of their meetings, lonely,
as usual, seething discreetly for country
and cause (as I saw it), I stayed in the still
long evenings, questioning, questioning. Scant days

later I left for Paris. The day
of the tyrant was almost done! That thought stayed
as I learned the intricate alleys, intrigues still
stunning Paris, the last-
ing rumors, riots, wrenching divisions, the country
a bloodied bath. But I was lonely,

worked dreams the lonely
plot, nights and days
for my country,
country I wanted once more staid
as Caen at childhood twilight. I wrote him at last
for audience. Still-

ness my answer. Raging still,
alone, no longer lonely,
I flung down two francs for a knife, almost the last
act in my play. And slept like a dove. Day
of vision and vindication! I stayed
him with promises, names of country-

men...knifed *his* country still in one second.
Lifting chaste skirts, I left him to her lonely soppings. This
last day, I dream back to visions: haymows,
    wildflowers....

POEM FOR ANNETTE VALLON, FRENCH MISTRESS OF WORDSWORTH, WHO SIGNED HERSELF "MADAME WILLIAM" FOR THE REST OF HER LIFE

It's easy to understand: a man facile
of tongue, an *English* tongue, nobody's vassal

obviously, obviously proud and, Mon Dieu!
a *poet*, romantically handsome, triste (un peu)

so you needed to comfort (the mystique of mother
in us all), and—ah, you were young; other

swains (mere boys) paled. I sense the lane
you walked together electric with berry-scent, mullein,

birds, his natural element, see you succumb
in a wily play of light and shade. I come

to the hurt of you later, William departed for peace,
pen and daffodils in England, while you piece

together tatters of your life. You had a child,
his, born in Christmastide's fragrant wild.

Had is the black bat whirring, worrying into wreaths
of greenery decayed, frost-edged as the far heaths

you write to, piteously. *My baby, they've taken her.*
Small town stuff, fat with pointing fingers: you're

a whore, your union's unblessed by the church, chalice
of mercy. No. We can't say it was malice,

excision of your heart like a cancer. Kind, shall we say
it was ignorance? Which is rarely bliss. See the way

ignorance still has dirty hands, nails
black with old, old blood. Annette, sails

never brought William back to you, but that craft,
time (not always seaworthy), did, like a raft

out of hopeless waters, give you back Caroline, teasing,
clapping, laughing, sun-dancing Caroline, easing

at least part of your pain. Sister, as I write
Christ's Mass candles flame again. By their light

I read your words, "The affection I have for her
will drive me mad...." This when you *hadn't* her.

I am not thinking *gifts*, or *The Gift*,
but of you alone in blue snow, ill-starred, adrift.

PHILLIS WHEATLEY: SOLILOQUY

Memory moves in the mind like moon on water,
seeming stilled yet slowly taking time,
light on the surface, dark in depths. Slaughter

by separation. I thought that cleaving crime
was graved forever under the headstone's message,
"Look forward. No eyes are placed behind." Time

unraveling to nothing before I age,
bones click back to forests, spuming flowers
like rainbow chips, far drums, exuberant foliage,

clearings coursing to sands flicked by showers
of sea like mirrors tinted mauve, blue,
green, the spectrum. Memory overpowers

now, that slept these busy years. New
sun spins up the sky. Clear as glass
I see my Mother, smiling, hands all sinew,

pouring water early over grass,
libation to her rising sun that in
my going set. I see her face, a mass

of crucifixion and my own its twin.
I will not let my senses sink to slave-ship,
gangrenous wound, nor to my sale, which sin

crazed all pillars of my soul. The trip
to Boston was a chatter of chills. Snow
stung all my sight, so like it was to slip

of sands white-hot at home to sea. Slow,
at first, but quicker with each moon, I learned
new ways and tongue and never let them know

my ache when they so kindly said I'd earned
their name, who had my *own* in ceremony
proudly given by our great Chief. I'd learned

the sense of silence, and they were kind, you see,
and forward looking. They sent me off to school.
Though I was a slave, they educated me.

In words I found my world, endless spool
of syllables for spinning to my style
all others' if I wished. Nor was she cool,

my Mistress, to my weaving. "How you beguile
with words," she said on reading. "Go on with this.
A talent takes fine honing." I reconcile

Its loss with what was gained: a trip, wild bliss,
to England, reception by their gracious Chief,
George Washington, in time a lover's lusty kiss

that made me wife. I hold a full-flowered sheaf,
though poor and ill, of retrospect. Reprise
rue-stemmed sways strong above its rooted grief.

"Night's leaden sceptre seals my drowsy eyes,
Then cease, my song, till fair Aurora rise."

II. 1600 A.D.
TO ABOUT 751 A.D.

SOLILOQUY: MRS. MAGDALEN HERBERT
MONTGOMERY CASTLE, WALES, 16—
ON RECEIVING AN EPISTLE FROM JOHN DONNE

He writes that once more he is seized
by melancholy. *And bluebells ecstatic*
on the hills! Why does he hear
in church bells only chimes
of death? I could see coal dust
shrouding trees, ponds, clouds
if I so positioned the compass
of my mind. I look to wings
slanting to clover, swans believing
in living tableaux. *John, John,*
you must practice what you preach. God
may be more simplistic than your blue
soundings. Stand by the Thames. See
how currents accommodate barges, birds,
islands of human muck in the mainstream.

How light falls into fleece. A servant
showed me this morning a new lamb.
Think of that, John. *Think of that*
as you swill in thoughts of suicide. Nightly
I watch the first star trembling over
these hills, think of its bright shadow
here, on my hand, *there*, on yours.

...Shall I pen him this
springspurt? How I want to
shake his bones to burning out
of his pit. *John, sun is ringing*
bluebells. The timbre of primroses
is promise. I wish you could hear
these crucibled sermons.

MADRIGAL FOR MARGARET RETRIEVING
THE HEAD OF SIR THOMAS MORE

How did she carry it, Margaret-his-daughter?
Catatonically, senses numb at the slaughter?
Piteously, pain cleaving to core?
Fastidiously, fingers flinching at gore?
Had she a monger's basket in hand?
Perhaps an old sack secured at some stand?
Or was the crock, heady with spices,
Under her cloak, preserved for this crisis?
Tenderly, surely, she claimed the dear head.
Did peace lighten night as she prayed by her bed?
Did she bear sorrow with joy as he taught her?
How *did* she carry it, Margaret-his-daughter?

LINES FOR HWANG CHIN-I
(1506-1544)

The sky is a silver dome this January night
like, perhaps, a silken robe you might
have worn composing a poem. What old light
we share, sister, caught in its necessary stream.
I walk the snow crust after reading of mountains.
Blue, you wrote, and, unlike love, unchanging.

You tinged love with philosophy, unchanging
thread through time and differing tongues. No night
of hurt was so dark your eyes missed mountains
fringing green in spring. Ache you might
for some forgotten him, but found a stream
of words you brushed to lyrical light.

In Songdo you were the point of light
admirers hovered round, fame's unchanging—
penalty? For what a poet wants is a stream
to dream beside, alone, a starred night
(like this), then silence, so muses can (or might,
with luck) dance, sing from mysterious mountains.

Somehow you wove your length of peace, mountains
offering shade, birds curving light
in air pine-and-peony-scented. Might
of warriors clanging near, you sang changes
of love and seasons against the night.
I hear them, this frosted night, thoughtful stream

of timbres. Geese in a flowing stream
cross the moon, blur its mountains.
Descendants, perhaps, of wild geese on a night
like this in your land? With ghostly light
they go, silent, lovely, in their unchanging
bodies a symbol of what endures beyond mighty

armies marching.... I think of how you might
gather them into a poem. Would they shadow a steam?
It shimmers before me, reeds at the edge unchanged
since your time, the pale rim of mountains
barely rippled in wind and tender light
dusking down as the first star opens night.

I move towards home under night's mighty dome,
dip my hand in the lighted stream, touch you
writing of mountains unchanged. Snow-flared. Splendid.

DIPTYCH: HARLINDE AND RENILDE, DAUGHTERS OF ALLARD, LORD OF DERAIN

With what foresight were they educated
in a convent at Valenciennes
centuries past when women were not fated,
(so men thought) to respond to learning?

With what foresight did they then renounce
the world that would not allow women's flashing minds
to flare beyond needlework's tame bounds?
See them at work in a nunnery at Maas-Eyck

writing, painting, deftly illuminating
the evangeliary found in the sacristy.
Listen to legend: while they were translating
inspiration to vellum by evening light

and wax-light, a cloud overcame them; a demon blew
the candles dark. Can you hear, through time
and civilization's bloody clamors, blue
night shutting down the world, miraculously,

the whispered breath of the Holy Spirit winking
wax-lights on, round each a radiant halo?
And the work goes on. Are you thinking
how demons and miracles were needed to explain

two gifted women's work? Still, we have it,
brilliant on the page, surviving both,
exposing both, the quiet, earnest grit
that gives us pale white doves, their moving shadows.

THE "ADA" SCHOOL

First great school
of the Carolingian Renaissance,
we read.

Who was Ada?
By what guttering light
did she bend eyes to art's rebirth,
rags catching
her monthly shed blood,
love, found or lost,
twisting gut and heart?

A sister of Charlemagne,
some say,
who sought a nunnery's peace.

No. Unscholarly,
others say, christening this school,
now, the "Rhineland School."

I'll still call it
"Ada"
and see an intense woman
walking through early morning grasses,
dew wetting her hem,
to the intricacies
of pestled colors, immaculate golds,
illuminating words
we seek again and again
for validation,
for renewal.

III.BIBLICAL WOMEN—
FIRST CENTURY A.D.

MARY OF MAGDALA

How tears became a water
lapping Magdala. I saw
nets I knew, holes holding
sun, fishermen's ribald songs,
curses, *life*
in their hands' vivid muscles,
wild hair smelling like winds
in places seen in dreams
where people dance, swirl
barefoot, bangled, golden,
gemmed, till stars creep home.

I forgot the hovel
light forgot to visit,
forgot weary thrashings
of soiled clothes on rocks
worn as the women washing,
forgot begging, beatings.

Hands on hips, I swayed by
the winking fishermen,
lazed eyes down all their hungry loins.

With some of them I sailed
the sea of Galillee: hidden coves
near rushes where small creatures
sang for us, birds plucked lutes.

One painted tales
of city brilliance, streets
shined with shekels.
I followed him until
his painted tales
petered out.

Then the house,
the Pharisee, tears
that became water
first of dreams long past
then the dream to come
where I *would live*....

I broke the vial.
Filth flowed out
of clothes, bones too beaten.
I was dancing, dancing, dancing
where stars touched hands
with sun, moon, tolerant rain
that pulsed like prayer.

I never cut my hair,
the crown of it so light
and touched by wings.

TRIPTYCH: THREE MOTHERS

I. Of the Figure on the Cross to the Right

I didn't want to hear it. *Puffing up*
that hill, a neighbor rushed to tell me, hard up
for gossip, I guess. You know the happy way
"friends" love to give bad news, though they play
at hating to. *Who,* I asked, flicking
an imaginary lint-mote from my apron, slicking
back straggling hair as if I didn't know who.
But, what odds, let her give her gloating view
of him—and maybe, maybe, just once I'd be
wrong. *Your boy that used to come to see*
my kid, remember? After making sure I'd heard
she ducked eyes to the floor as if too stirred
to watch. *Sit down, Lena, have some wine.*
I pulled a half-drunk jug from the ragged line
of them. I run a little place, a bar,
sort of, couple beds upstairs—not particular
who sleeps with who, long as they pay me—first.
That Mary's been here with her guys. Cursed
me out, too, for dirty bedding. *Hell,*
I spat, *think this is Herod's palace?* Well
she shut up, tossed half-bare breasts, lured him
upstairs. The floor creaked soon (those frantic limbs).
Just half, Rachel. She watched like a ferret while
I filled her cup. Who's kidding. We both pile
it in like air. We each took slugs. *So?*
Why's he on the hill, why puffing? The glow
made her glib. *He's bent with a cross on his back,*
Rachel. Him and one other. God. They'll tack
him up for good this time. I always knew
he'd end up on a tree. She belched her brew
and gabbled on. *He's hairy like an ape,*
and heavy. Last time I saw him (it was rape,
that time, wasn't it, with a boy?)—she winked

and drooled, *he was young and slim, clinked*
gold coins in his pocket, on the bar. Oh
beautiful he was, and sang, low,
sweet. Charmed the room of us, those hags
you keep for gentlemen's comfort. Filthy rags;
as if he'd look at them. She laughed a gale.
My old cat whirled away, tipped a pail
of washwater. I boxed her ears. Lena's, I mean.
Hard. She stopped, gasped, lurched, obscene
and sodden. I drew myself up. *I don't know*
what he's done that's drawn him death. I owe
him nothing or he me. The knot's been cut
long years. I never see him. He twists my gut
no more. Good riddance. I hope they hammer sure
the killing nails. Get out; I'm busy. A caricature
of how she came, she left. I took my wine
sat, stared out the window. A sudden whine
of wind shook trees and house. The sky flared black,
and thundered. I lit no candle. Suddenly my back
crumpled, twisted with pain. No one came.
I writhed in the lonely dark, sobbing his name.

II. Of The Central Figure: Stabat Mater

A small wind. My eyes fill with a single
daisy bending slightly in the shallow dingle
to my right. Its eye meets mine, brooding, dark in its pure-
petalled setting, like a jewel devoid of sun's spark
blurred now by clouds melancholy as the magnetic eye
which becomes, as I stare, a window, the small one high
in the stable's sloping roof I drift through down,
down to the aromatic hay that cradled me, crown
of him thrusting, knocking through my thighs to life,
our entwined cries blending with animals'. No still life
stays that memory. Nothing of frieze about
it. An ass stomped, bellowed, the ox gave a shout

that fluttered pigeons from sleepy roosts, a mouse
skittered up my stomach, stopped as if stunned on my blouse
taut with bloated breasts till Joseph roared
its quivering away. Two bats, astonished, soared
startlingly close. It was all confusion until
my baby was safe in the crude byre, still
in the quieted barn. My husband brought me, then,
a sheaf of daisies gathered outside the wooden
door, eyes of them moist with dew. Like tears.
How wise the simple flowers that softened all fears
that night of rejection, hard birth in a rude
stall. I drifted to sleep in their fragrant prelude
to kind dreams where petals blurred to one point
of star like the one outside which seemed to anoint
my son's destiny. A clap of thunder knocks
me to now and the shaking hill. Wind lifts his locks
I loved to twine round my finger when he was small.
Such wild curls. So willful. He used to call
me silly and pull away, frowning—tenderly, always
tenderly. Oh on the terrible post he sways
straining against the nails I cannot blame,
innocent as he, pawns in the horror-filled game
of politics. *No. Not politics.* He corrected me
on the night we last spoke, I ranting, he
calm in his tranquil aura. *Beyond this world,*
Mother, I tell you as I've told them, whirled
on currented winds towards what I know. He sighed.
We said no more, silently side-by-side,
flesh-against-flesh, watched the full moon light
the garden, Gethsemane, where we'd come for sight,
he said, of night-blooming wildflowers growing only
there. We found none, but he wandered slowly
over rocks, among roots the moon made gold.
I stifled questions, sensing something told
before, long ago, he could not share
with even a loving mother. How it was rare,
our last bright communion. But his peace

has not found *me*. Not of this world? Least
comfort to a mother nailed to dailiness, earth,
and hard remembrance of *this* world, the mirth,
the known flesh of him. I cannot even wail,
hammered still, gored by the killing gale.

III. Of the Figure on the Cross to the Left

No one noticed me, in tatters, crippled,
my face a field of webs the stiff wind rippled.
And I came last, in my throat my breath
leaping like hooked fish. I thought sure death
would strangle me on the long steep hill I stumbled
up bent double to the breeze. I fumbled
over rock and root. You might have thought
my shoulders cradled a cross, that only sought
the summit. The three so burdened led the crowd
that jostled, spat, and ridiculed in loud
wine-tilted tones. I straggled, as I say,
eyes blurred with more than dust. Black clouds lay
upon the hill as I pushed closer. Beams,
already up and bodied, creaked in streams
of wind that stung like flung pebbles. I staggered
to the mount just left of center, haggard,
spent, weeping because I came too late
to kiss his face, his rock-cut feet, create
a last brief haven in my arms that held
him, small and squirming, to my breast. Eyes welled
with rage at age that slowed taut bones. Squinting
up the terrible post, lightning flinting
all the sky with fire, my eyes took blood,
my son's, for vision. Slumping, I saw a flood
of former scenes in that red swirl: the time
he toddled first, his first-tried words, grime
streaking his face at a kitten's loss, the nursed
bird he could not save; then the first
wild spree with friends not of our kind, the need

for coins beyond his power to earn; the deed
at last that drove him here too young. *He would
have changed in time, I know. Oh he is good,
good, another chance....* I beat deaf ground
till someone dragged me from the cross-marked mound.
But as I scraped across hard earth I heard
sob down the wind my son's dear voice; one word,
then two, so slow, so faint, "Remember me—"
Thunder took the rest. Then, "You will be,"
the words came haltingly, yet firm, "with me
in Paradise." Was it a dream? A sea
of mist spun round my senses. Stunned, I peered
through blackness, through the deadly wind that veered
all ways at once and saw through sudden light
it was the one in thorns who spoke. Right
and might and something more, far more, lay on
his features pain incised. My son was gone,
I saw, drained pale and slack. I stared, all need
for weeping done, stilled by the whispered creed
come from above, and then I threw my face
down on the bloody, stony, hallowed place
in fear, for I knew they had hanged a King
not of this world, just as He said. A thing
beyond men's vision swayed tacked and torn. I prayed,
while hell crashed everywhere, afraid, afraid.

IV.ABOUT 1200 B.C.

AFTERMATH

I.
Still I remember Colonus. There to greet
my desolate father and sister, the pungent sweet

fragrance of grapes nevertheless seized
my senses, as did the querulous hum of bees.

Listen, there is the almost liquid tap-
tap of olive against olive, the snap

of twigs under our feet as we walked in the shadow
of cypresses twisted with old tales, no

strangers to loss and grief. I remember sun
dappling through, shawling us, a benison.

Place of Benignant Goddesses, sacred to them,
it became sacred to us, a refuge. Earth's hem

knew my kisses. And Antigone's. Though blind,
Oedipus vowed he could see the welcoming kind

grove, the dipping, uplifting birds. I'd come
to tell good news of the comforting oracle. Wearisome

long wanderings ended in relief clear
on my father's face. His were joyous tears!

Here in my eye is the scented glen, the moon
full on my father's happy final swoon

into death and all beyond it. A long time
we held him, Antigone and I, till rime

touched his beard, our grieving hearts, and we
were sent home, away from the heady, lovely

sacred site which has never left my sight.
Yes. I remember Colonus, its offered light.

the echo of wind in old trees

II.
What do we owe a brother?
Oh Polyneices, wherever you are,
do you know how that question's branded
on every bone in my body?
How I've answered
     life itself
I still living? Living my gift of horror.

the rasp of storm-tossed limbs

III.
After her death I left by boat
in the middle of the night. An old tub
abandoned at water's edge, one broken
oar alone mocking me. I sank
out of my senses, drifted at last
to an island, few inhabitants, no
questions about a white-haired hag
(so I'd become, I saw in a pool),
frail and poor, washed up, they thought,
from some shipwreck. Nothing unusual
on that isolated island. They helped me find
a hut, offered figs, olives,
wine, tattered bedding, homespun
for my almost naked bones,
bones bent under the burden,
the warmth of heaped kindnesses
I did not deserve.

Better to have died,
I'd howl in my hut, nights alone,
and thought how I could

die. A clutch of vine
around my throat, it looped
to a tree? The sea itself
I'd walk into, never
looking back? Berries,
some slow poison, I needing
to know a long, long agony?

What do we owe a brother?

I had no courage, even for that,
weighted with the longest agony,
the incessant, piercing
death, daily.

      the darkness of beach shells at midnight

IV.
I'm not young. It can't be
much longer that I drag
to the small village, watch
dancers on a festive night,
see lovers born anew
in candle-lit wine,
in each other's eyes,
hear lyres hauntingly,
hear people greet me
lovingly out of respect
for the old. When I weep
(though I've gone to the country
far beyond that, mostly)
they pat and cuddle, think
it's for my family lost
at sea, I the sole survivor.

O my father, O my sister

O my dearest brother,
it is I who was, am,
left for beasts and birds
to tear at and devour
over and over again,
I the unburied soul
though I died long ago.

the sour wine, the snuffed candles

V.
It is sunrise. Another day. Rays
find all corners of my hut, play

on cornered webs gently plucked by wind.
There is singing. Amethyst and opaline

the sea spills its ancient jewels on the strand.
It is Antigone singing. I am in the land

of our shared childhood. Polyneices strings
a kite skyward. Laughing, I follow him. A gull wings

old messages, carries us on its back
to Colonus, the sacred place. Here we lack

nothing. There is the music of cypresses moving
sedately, grey-green olive leaves turning, saying

what they know. We are a family, one
against all the world. I lie down, undone

by beauty, pity, the reaching-out arms of a brother.
He rocks me to sleep. My brother, O my brother.

And the sea understands, holds tales,
bones, washes still all anguished wails.

ABISHAG: RECOLLECTIONS IN OLD AGE

I have known horrors.
          There was the spring ice
covered desert roses,
fields before they could offer food,
beasts as they stiffened
like a frieze in the temple.
We ate dirt
ground
with water and baked.
Our bodies curled
into themselves, wormlike,
and withered.

          Two summers after
they came for me,
heat eating earth like locusts the grass,
seas running languid over sands.

          "The King has need of you."

I, fourteen summers blooming
my virgin body,
obeyed the summoning, a chosen child.

They spoke of cold
          chattering his bones
                    like currents in a cavern.
(I heard them whisper of my young warmth).
What illness was it?
I couldn't ask.

Soon, I saw.
His bed domed a dais
canopied and jeweled.

He lay swaddled, swathed in skins,
his own like webs on stone.
His eyes were sunk to winter pools and oozed
rheum.

        I lay with him.

Kind David, singer of songs, sang,
voice cracked and quavering,
        of my hair like night's long threads
        I wound him in;
        of my breasts like rare white birds
        and warmer
        fairer then Bathsheba's in remembrance;
        of my lips like sun-licked silphium.

I, autumn half over,
see
his still tucked manhood
whorled like a snail,
feel
the slab of his loins
the crack of his bones like
ice,
the shaking, fumbling, fragile, frigid
fingers...
        He never knew me.

HELEN: THE DARK INTERIOR

There were treasures in Troy.
Fruit faceted the garden
in my private grounds:
figs, currants, the subtler
lemons, pungent orangetrees
in a frieze stately
edged the pool that drew me
daily to its glass.

Kneeling, my girdle knotted
round my waist and a stout
unyielding trunk, I slipped
swanlike my scented breasts,
neck, and perfect face
over tilting birds,
idling clouds, the mass
of fertile fruit dark-shadowed
in that shining. Beauty
was my beast, a murderer
I knew and could not kill
by fracturing with fists
day after day in that
still pool that cooly eased
to smooth the maze of lines
scored and pummeled on
my face.

You see I heard of her,
Iphigenia, slain
to still roiled winds so ships
might sail for me—for *me*,
whose skin would craze like a vase
slipped from time's slack fingers.
It was a white gull told me,
come through storm to nest.
Self-loathing settled like

a blight, though I pretended
lust, and perfumed loins.
He never saw the rites
perfected at the pool.

It was Astyanax
burned bones black, scarred
forever the face that launched
the slow sad ships. "So fair,
worth all," I heard men whisper
as I boarded. "Blind,"
I clamored in my head,
"to death pocks and eyes' empty
holes winds wail through, deaf
to his cries twisting up
the keen-edged cliff in gales
of innocent grief, stabbing,
ripping, knifing, skin."

We sail for Greece, my face
dark with Troy's fine ash.
I set my teeth and smile,
like sun, a body, burning.

ONE OF THE SUITORS' HARLOTS

New pomade from the traders,
heavy-scented, not like musk, nothing
known before, sweet, not cloying.
I dress each nipple in it,
silk all other space more subtly.
One lures by less,
and lust's unstable.

Eurykleia's voice like flint:
Odysseus home in hall, hungry
for slaves the suitors knew!
Here's homespun. I fumble, mumble.
Will it hide, or simple, scent?
I quake through cold corridors
to—a bloody Lord, a lion
still as a storm contained
barely, about him, everywhere,
corpses strewn like pallid pelts.

Carnage, carnage! While I laved
loins, thought of a probing rod
inside me like fire, cries, howls,
death tones arrowed air.
I was away in memory moving seas
far from this place, nudging sands
not ever seen before by any lovers,
heard only gossamer gulls, jeweled
voices shimmering, gliding down
mauve skies to facet secret seas....

"Harlots!"
His sound slits reverie. I tumble
out my supper, adding to the entrails
streaming in putrid heaps, my love's
beside his hacked-off head flies foul.

"Make them—" I fall into darkness someone
waters away. A sponge is thrust, a gesture cracks
glazed disbelief. Clean—*this?*
Stinking hangings, stark-
open eyes recording all, tongues
stuck out in deadly taunt?

I cannot

I stand, a propped-up corpse
they prod, shove; I squint
to halve the sight, and,
a barque spun mad in wind,
tremble to the impossible, Odysseus
staring, stony, terrible.

*

The thing is done. No sound
can tell you how. I,
sleek-scented limbs garishly
gore-stockinged, am herded out
with others. I gasp changed air,
choked by Death's veins
hideously leaking.

We huddle close,
horror, shame, our tattered clothes,
dazed,
watch Telemakhos rope the roundhouse top
to a strong pillar.
Even numb, we know
this game. We are to be strung up
like silly sheep. My voice
spears air, again, again, again. I think,

frenzied moments before whirling
free in space, of singing
nights that hoist me here, of his fool organ
filling me like flaring stars, breasts
lying in wait for him, the crazy, slippery
stupid clutching
                    one small white flower
through stone cracks fills my whole seeing.
I water it to death.

AFTERWORD

I was fortunate to have been born into a family where words and music made up the air we breathed. Books filled our house in a happy jumble, along with various instruments and scores. Both parents were musicians, my mother a graduate of The London College of Music. My father, a clergyman, had a silver tongue and often quoted poetry in his sermons. He gave readings in the old sense: from memory. My three sisters and two brothers all have been active in the arts.

Odd, then, perhaps, that I did not come to the writing of poetry until the age of 45, though I have read it omnivorously all my life, as others read novels. I seem to have come to many things late! Earned both an undergraduate and a Master's degree while raising my three sons. Then, at long last, it was my turn. Perhaps the long delay was in part why I was drawn to writing about the lives of women, for women so often sublimate their needs and dreams to the demands of others. I am attracted to the persona poem, the Dramatic Monologue; it is a challenge to me to attempt to get into the minds and hearts of various people, in the case of this collection, specifically women. I was moved to attempt to retrieve some who have been relegated to footnotes or only a page or two in the biographies of men.

Several of these women were ruthlessly, cruelly, abandoned, a circumstance as timely today as in their eras. Ira Dalser, for instance, Mussolini's mistress, was imprisoned in a lunatic asylum simply to get her out of the dictator's way Annette Vallon piteously retained Wordsworth's name throughout the rest of her life. Marie d'Agoult, Liszt's mistress (one of them!) and the mother of his children, suffered greatly, but was able to summon the strength to write scathingly of the musician's defection. Olive Schreiner's *The Story of an African Farm* is a classic ralying call to women to develop independent lives; its pictures of the karroo speak to us today as we daily read of the unspeakable conditions inSouth Africa. Each woman I wrote about appealed to me in varying ways. Here are lives I felt deserved exposure to more light. Many of them have never before been addressed in poetry. I wanted to bring them into the canon.

As for the art of poetry itself, simply, I love it, almost sensuously love words. I enjoy working in both traditional forms and free verse, just as, if one is going to be a serious pianist, one learns to play in all keys. Beyond that, far beyond that, is what is being said. I have never believed that "poetry makes nothing happen." I think it can make *everything* happen (pace Auden, writing of my revered countryman), in that most important place, the interior life, which shapes the outer, which shapes the world.

NOTES TO THE POEMS:
*Since writing "For Jacqueline du Pré," she has died.
*Ida Dalser was Mussolini's mistress and mother of his son, Benito.
*Suzanne Valadon, mother of Utrillo, died of a stroke while painting.
*"Reminiscences: Victorious Life, Olive Schreiner," is taken from her classic work, *The Story of an African Farm.*
*"Two Stalks in a Garden," On Jane Wells and Rebecca West, was first published in *Shenandoah* as "Triptych," the third figure being, of course, H.G. Wells. (The third stalk, to carry out the metaphor).
*Mathilde was Mary Cassatt's faithful servant for forty years.
*Marie d'Agoult, mother of Liszt's three children, had to publish her novel *Nelida* under the pseudonym Daniel Stern.
*The Final couplet in "Phillis Wheatley: Soliloquy" is from her "An Hymn to Evening."
*Germaine Greer notes in *The Obstacle Race* that *The ACTA*
Sanctorum Bollandorum indicates that Harlinde and Renilde mastered the arts of writing and painting, "a task laborious even to men."!
*Hwang Chin-I, according to a Korean anthology was "the most famous and the most accomplished of all Korean women poets."
*In Edith Hamilton's *Mythology* "Ismene disappears. There is no story, no poem about her."

for Patricia Lea Fairchild

The local is not a place but a place in a given man—what part of it he has been compelled or else brought by love to give witness to in his own mind. And that is THE form, that is, the whole thing, as whole as it can get.
—Robert Creeley

B.H. FAIRCHILD

Local Knowledge

B.H. FAIRCHILD was born in Houston, Texas in 1942 and grew up there and in small towns in Oklahoma, west Texas, and southwestern Kansas. Educated at the University of Tulsa and University of Kansas, he has worked as a machinist's helper, movie usher, musician, and technical writer, and is currently a professor of English at California State University in San Bernardino, where he resides with his wife and two children. His study of William Blake, *Such Holy Song*, appeared in 1980, and his books of poems include *C&W Machine Works*, *Flight*, *The Arrival of the Future*, and *The System of Which the Body is One Part*. He has been the recipient of several awards including the Seaton Poetry Award, the AWP Anniversary Award, and most recently, an NEA Fellowship.

CONTENTS

**PART ONE: THE STRUCTURES
OF EVERYDAY LIFE**

The Structures of Everyday Life	8
Speaking the Names	9
Language, Nonsense, Desire	11
The Doppler Effect	12
The Messengers	13
Fire and Water	14
Kansas	16
Maize	17
The Machinist, Teaching His Daughter to Play the Piano	18

PART TWO: HISTORY

Toban's Precision Machine Shop	21
In a Cafe near Tuba City, Arizona	23
West Texas	25
Michael Blum Cuts His Brother's Hair	26
Strength	27
The Last Days	28
Photograph of a College Football Team, 1927	29
Soliloquy of the Appliance Repairman	31
Saipan	32

**PART THREE: THE SYSTEM OF WHICH
THE BODY IS ONE PART**

There Is Constant Movement in My Head	35
The Drunk Foreman	37
Angels	38
Sheets	39
Work	40
The City of God	43
The Woman at the Laundromat Crying "Mercy"	45
December, 1986	46
The Robinson Hotel	47

PART FOUR: IN CZECHOSLOVAKIA

In Another Life I Encounter My Father   49
L'Attente   51
Child and Dwarf   52
Local Knowledge   54
My Mother's Dreams   61
The March of the Suicides   63
In Czechoslovakia   64
Dust Storm   67

AFTERWORD: LATHEWORK   69

PART ONE:
THE STRUCTURES
OF EVERYDAY LIFE

THE STRUCTURES OF EVERYDAY LIFE

In the shop's nave, where the wind bangs sheets
of tin against iron beams, barn sparrows
quarrel like old lovers. At five o'clock
the lathes wind down from their long flight.
Burnt coils of steel loom from collecting bins.

In the wash room photographs of wives and lovers
look down on the backs of men pale as shells.
Brown wrists and black hands lather and shine
in the light of one dim lamp, and blue shirts
hang like the stilled hands of a deaf-mute.

When the foreman sees his raw face in the mirror,
he turns away, shy as a young girl, sick of iron
and rust, the dead sun of the day's end. After
washing, his wet hair gleams in the open door
and he begins his dream of women in cool rooms.

Gusts seep through tin, making the thin music
the men live by. Drill pipe they scar knuckles on
clangs restless as planets on the rack outside.
The ten-ton hoist drags its death chain. The sky
is a gray drum, a dull hunger only the plains know.

Like children at prayer, the men kneel to lace
their shoes, touching the worn heels of a life.
When they leave, the faces on their locker doors
turn back to darkness. Each man shoulders the sun,
carries it through the fields, the lighted streets.

SPEAKING THE NAMES

When frost first enters the air
in the country of moon and stars,
the world has glass edges, and the hard glint
of crystals seeping over iron
makes even the abandoned tractor seem all night sky
    and starlight.

On the backporch taking deep breaths like some miracle cure,
breathe, let the spirit move you,
here I am after the long line of cigarettes
that follows grief like a curse, trying to breathe, revive,
in this land of revivals and lost farms . . .

It is no good to grow up hating the rich.
In spring I would lie down among pale anemone and primrose
and listen to the river's darkening hymn, and soon
the clouds were unravelling like the frayed sleeves of field
    hands,
and ideology had flown with the sparrows.

The cottonwood that sheltered the hen house is a stump now,
and the hackberries on the north were leveled years ago.
Bluestem hides the cellar, with its sweet gloom of clay walls
    and bottles.
The silo looms over the barn, whose huge door swallowed
    daylight,
where a child could enter his own death.

What became of the boy with nine fingers?
The midwife from Yellow Horse who raised geese?
They turned their backs on the hard life,

and from the tree line along the river they seem to rise now,
her plain dress bronze in moonlight, his wheatshock hair
    in flames.

Behind me is a house without people. And so, for my sake
I bring them back, watching the quick cloud of vapor that
    blooms
and vanishes with each syllable: *O.T.* and *Nellie Swearingen,*
their children, *Locie, Dorrel, Deanie, Bill,*
and the late *Vinna Adams,* whose name I speak into the bright
    and final air.

LANGUAGE, NONSENSE, DESIRE

Professor Ramirez dozes behind the projector,
Conversación Español lapping over the bored
shoulders of sophomores who dissolve in the film's
languor of talk and coffee at a sidewalk cafe
in Madrid or Barcelona or some other luminous
Mediterranean dream. The tanned faces rounding
into the Spanish air like bowls of still-life fruit
offer little dialogues about streetcars or feathers
over a clutter of plates and delicate white cups
of mocha blend. The hands of the speakers
are bright birds that lift and tremble among
the anomalies of ordinary life: *piñatas*, cousins
who live in Peru, the last train to Zaragoza.
The speakers are three friends forever entangled
in the syntax of Spanish 101, fated to shape
loose chatter into harmonies of discourse, arias
of locus, *¿Dónde esta la casa?* and possession,
Yo tengo un perro: Raoul, his dark, hungry
profile immaculately defined against the pallor
of a white beach; the housewife Esmeralda erotic
in her onyx curls, recalling a Catholic childhood,
that same black extravagance pressed against
her pillow as she listened to the nun read stories
and imagined herself as a *gaucho*, drunk and love-
crazed in the hills of Argentina; and wan Julio,
articulate, epicene, fluttering his pianist's fingers
as he croons melodiously about the rush of time:
¿Qué hora es? ¿Son las dos? ¡Ay! And always
in the background along the periphery of syllable
and gesture, the silent pilgrimage of traffic
and commerce and light-dazzled crowds with some
destination, some far blue promise to carry them
through the day, some end to speech and love.

THE DOPPLER EFFECT

When I would go into bars in those days
the hard round faces would turn
to speak something like loneliness
but deeper, the rain spilling into gutters
or the sound of a car pulling away
in a moment of sleeplessness just before dawn,
the Doppler effect, I would have said shrewdly then,
of faces diminishing slightly into the distance
even as they spoke. Their children
were doing well, somewhere, and their wives
were somewhere, too, and we were here
with those yellow euphoric flowers
unfolding slowly in our eyes
and the sun which we had not seen for days
nuzzling our fingertips and licking
our elbows. Oh, it was all there, and
there again the same, our heads nodding,
hands resting lightly upon the mahogany sheen
of the bar. Then one of us would leave
and the door would turn to a yellow square
so sudden and full of fire
that our eyes would daze and we would
stare into the long mirrors for hours
and speak shrewdly of that pulling away,
that going toward something.

THE MESSENGERS

At twilight baseball fields make their green cries
of abandonment, the dust lying still on the base paths,
the outfield thick with the secrets of mushrooms.

On Crosstown 30 Louise Johnson is hauling
baseball trophies in her pickup.
They gleam like the backs of dolphins
or rows of votive candles flickering in the half-light.
They are Brahmin, the red dot of the sun is on their foreheads.

Louise points her cigar toward the horizon,
the little bronze men press on, shoulder to shoulder.
They plunge through the failed landscape—
the housing tracts, the smog's death-shroud, the stolen water
of the Los Angeles aqueduct:
                                        Receive us,
let us be among the earth's children
who await the withheld promise, the floating fast ball,
the fat knuckler that turns like a distant planet.

The entire Little League is mad with desire.
Flood lights shatter the darkness,
the shouts of lost fathers litter the diamond.
In the monastic silences of right field, thin arms
and a glove wide as a moon are raised against the ball's
        long arc.

Here comes Louise, pickup clattering
like an exhausted army, her left arm lifted
toward the indifferent sky. Cities lie swollen
with lights along the valley. Statuettes are waiting
to be born. In our dreams, children are praying.

FIRE AND WATER

Old girl. She mumbled like an idle child,
clapping, endlessly babbling, *the fire,*
the house, ankle-deep in slush, junk
bludgeoned with smoke, blasted by fire-hoses.
Oh, if things could only die, she sobbed,
collecting the wounded: porcelain angel
statuettes smudged and gloomy as fog now;
charred clumps of photos like fat beetles;
the WW II souvenir silk pillow, a brown wad
jammed beneath the still steaming couch.
Things, marginalia of a house, a life
between walls hung with hand-work, knitted
shawls and quilts where now what was left of
wallpaper drooped blistered and fringed
in brown scallops.
                                    Fire and water:
flames sluicing over window sills, bleeding
around corners lurid as snake weed
from the trampled side yard; afterward,
black tide-pools, thick soup of memory,
a wrecked lamp stranded like a crane
in a drained lake. Each day I trundled
sludge and garbage from the drowned house,
and each night she rose from the one
untouched bed and slipped into the alley,
lifted piles of rubble under the ragged
shawl of moonlight, then lugged them in
and stumbled back for more. One night
she banged a ruined hatrack through
the gutted kitchen, and I woke
to bellow in her dumb ears, *It's trash,*

shit, leave it! Truckloads kept
coming back, kept haunting my burnt-out
mornings until I gave up.

                    I stocked
the new apartment with kitchen ware, copper
pans and big skillets bright as moons.
The white tile floor shone like glazed ice,
the yellow wall paint still too wet
to touch. We stood together at the sink
washing our hands and peering down
at the pool raging in the flames of noon
and cries of swimmers bruising the air.
How young they were! and how beautiful,
with their bright, anonymous faces and
their hands raised, as if pushing something
back, and their lean bodies just lightly
scorched by the diminishing fire of the sun.

KANSAS

Leaning against my car
after changing the oil,
I hold my black hands out
and stare at them as if they were the faces
of my children looking at the winter moon
and thinking of snow that is promised,
that will erase everything before they wake.

In the garage, my wife
comes behind me and slides her hands
beneath my soiled shirt.
Pressing her face between my shoulder blades,
she mumbles something, and soon
we are laughing and wrestling
like children among shadows and old rags:

towels that unravel endlessly,
mounds of torn sheets, work shirts
from twenty years ago when I stood
in the door of my father's shop,
grease-blackened, and Kansas lay before me
blazing with new snow, a future
of flat land and sunlight.

After making love,
we lie on the abandoned mattress
and stare at our pale winter bodies
sprawling in the half-light.
She touches her belly, the scar
of our last child, and the black
prints of my hands along her hips and thighs.

MAIZE

After Roland Stills fell from the top of the GANO
grain elevator, we felt obliged in some confused,
floundering way as if his hand had just pulled
the red flag from our pockets and we had turned
to find not him but rows of Kansas maize
reeling into the sun, we felt driven to recall
more than perhaps, drunk, we saw: trees squatting
below like pond frogs, mare's tails sweeping the hills,
and the moon in its floppy dress riding low behind
the shock of his yellow hair as, falling, he seemed
to drop to his knees, drunk, passing out, *oh shit*,
with the same stupid grin as when he might recite
Baudelaire in the company of a girl and a small glass
of Cointreau, *Je suis comme le roi d'un pays pluvieux.*
And beyond his eyes blooming suddenly into white
flowers were the lights of houses where our parents
spoke of harvest like a huge wall they would climb
to come again to a new life. Driving along dirt roads
in our trucks, we would look through the scrim of dust
at the throbbing land and rows of red maize whipping past
before the hard heat of summer when the combines
came pushing their shadows and shouldering each other
dark as clouds erasing the horizon, coming down
on the fields to cut the maize, to cut it down
in a country without rain or the grace of kings.

THE MACHINIST, TEACHING HIS DAUGHTER
TO PLAY THE PIANO

The brown wrist and hand with its raw knuckles and blue nails
    packed with dirt and oil, pause in mid-air,
the fingers arched delicately,

and she mimics him, hand held just so, the wrist loose,
    then swooping down to the wrong chord.
She lifts her hand and tries again.

Drill collars rumble, hammering the nubbin-posts.
    The helper lifts one, turning it slowly,
then lugs it into the lathe's chuck.

The bit sheers the dull iron into new metal, falling
    into the steady chant of lathe work,
and the machinist lights a cigarette, holding

in his upturned palms the polonaise he learned at ten,
    then later the easiest waltzes,
etudes, impossible counterpoint

like the voice of his daughter he overhears one night
    standing in the backyard. She is speaking
to herself but not herself, as in prayer,

the listener is some version of herself
    and the names are pronounced carefully,
self-consciously: Chopin, Mozart,

Scarlatti . . . these gestures of voice, and hands
    suspended over the keyboard
that move like the lathe in its turning

toward music, the wind dragging the hoist chain, the ring
    of iron on iron in the holding rack.
His daughter speaks to him one night,

but not to him, rather someone created between them,
    a listener, there and not there,
a master of lathes, a student of music.

PART TWO: HISTORY

There is a history slower still than the history of civilizations, a history which almost stands still, a history of man in his intimate relationship to the earth which bears and feeds him; it is a dialogue which never stops repeating itself, which repeats itself in order to persist, which may and does change superficially, but which goes on, tenaciously, as though it were somehow beyond time's reach and ravages.
                                        Fernand Braudel

TOBAN'S PRECISION MACHINE SHOP

It has just rained, a slow movement of Mahler
drifts from Toban's office in back, the windows
blurred by runnels of grease and dirt, and I walk
into the grease-and-water smell like a child
entering his grandmother's closet. It is a shop
so old the lathes are driven by leather belts
descending like some spiritual harness
from a long shaft beneath the tin roof's peak.

Such emptiness. Such a large and palpable
sculpture of disuse: lathes leaning against
their leather straps, grinding wheels motionless
above mounds of iron filings. Tools lie lead-
heavy along the backs of steel workbenches,
burnished where the morning light leaks through
and lifts them up. Calipers and honing cloths
hang suspended in someone's dream of perfection.

There are times when the sun lingers over
the green plastic panels on the roof, and light
seems to rise from the floor, seems to lift lathes
and floor at once, and something announces itself:
not beauty, but rather its possibility,
and you almost reach out, almost lean forward
to lie down in that wash of bronze light, as if
it would bear you up, would hold you in sleep.

Wasn't this our secret dream, to lie down in work,
to bathe in the common light of our labor
as if work were a kind of prayer, as if the loss
of hours could be redeemed, and I would unfold

my arms, fingers spread wide, and the other
machinists would do the same, until the art
of levitation had become as precise
as iron curling under the edge of a steel bit?

Toban no longer sees the shop advancing
into its day's purchase of light and dark.
He sits in his office among his books
with music settling down on his shoulders
like a warm shawl. He replaces the Mahler
with Schubert, the B flat sonata, and sends it
unravelling toward me, turning the sound
far above the cluttered silence of the lathes.

IN A CAFE NEAR TUBA CITY, ARIZONA,
BEATING MY HEAD AGAINST A CIGARETTE MACHINE

> *...the sea shall give up her dead; and the*
> *corruptible bodies of those who sleep in*
> *him shall be changed, and made like unto*
> *his glorious body.*
> —The Book of Common Prayer

The ruptured Pontiac, comatose and tilted on three wheels,
seems to sink slowly like a drunken ship into the asphalt.
My wife wanders aimlessly farther into despair and an absence
of traffic, waving invisible semaphores along the embankment.
The infant we have misnamed after a suicidal poet writhes
in harness across my back, her warm urine funneling between
my buttocks, and her yowls rip like sharks through
    the grey heat.
But still beyond the screams I hear somehow the flutter
    and thrum
of chicken wings, buckets rattling, the howl of spaniels,
and my grandfather's curse grinding against the dull, unjust sky
of God and Oklahoma. I have given the waitress all my money,
and she has taken it, stuffed it into the heart-shaped pocket
monogrammed with her ridiculous name, and removed herself
to the storeroom with the cook who wants only to doze through
the mid-afternoon lull undisturbed by a man who has yanked
    the PALL
MALL knob from the cigarette machine and now beats his head
    against
the coin return button while mumbling the prayer for the Burial
of the Dead at Sea which his grandmother taught him as a charm
against madness in the long silences before tornadoes and floods
when Black Bear Creek rose on the Oto and the windmill began
to shriek like a gang of vampires. In the shards of the machine's
mirror I see the black line of blood dividing my forehead

and a dozen versions of my wife sobbing now at the screen door while behind her our laundry has flown free of the Pontiac's wired trunk lid and drifts like gulls across the vast sea, the difficult sea surrounding Tuba City, Arizona, and my grandparents walk slowly toward us over the water in the serene and noble attitude of gods.

WEST TEXAS

My red Ford running to rust idles
along the roadside, one headlight
swinging out across the plains,
the other blind. In the rear window
dawn light spills over my children
sprawling tangled in the back seat
beneath an army blanket. My wife
sleeps in front where the radio loses
itself in static, and even Del Rio
is a distant shout. From rig
to rig like this every few months,
sometimes sooner, the road looming
toward more sky, bunch grass, hard
angry limbs of mesquite. Always
a thin gauze of dirt in the air.
Coffee blackens through the night,
and now I spill the grounds like seeds
from another country over the dry
shoulder. Driving high and sleepless,
I dream awake: faces like strange
black flowers form and vanish,
my father stooping in the road, then
looking up. *Stay put, let the land
claim you,* he always said. But here
men own you and the land you drill,
and you move on. My one headlight
shooting out of line across West Texas
dims in the morning light. The other
mirrors back the road, the whitening
sky, my tired eyes. A hawk is sweeping
into view on wide, black wings.

MICHAEL BLUM CUTS HIS BROTHER'S HAIR

Hair and leaves fall together under the cottonwood,
under the wide eaves behind our mother's house
where Karl, a huge man whose life in steel and iron
has ruined his hands with bruises, sits slumped,
legs crossed like a girl's, and watches red locks
sweep across the sheet that laps over his knees.
They are quiet as women folding precious linens
and have not spoken to each other in seven years.

In a gray stubble field where dust devils whipped across
wire fences, our brothers came to blows over
land and money and rightful shares. Then they fell
to silence, two boarded houses standing side by side,
one red truck beside a black at Neiderland's Cafe
on weekday mornings. But from boyhood, Mike, the elder,
did the family barbering, and now we watch the hair
fall and drift across dry leaves and yellow grass.

As the wind picks up and the branches sway and scrape
like blown papers, Mike hums his song, and the words
rise secretly in our minds, *Meine Ruh ist hin, Mein Herz
ist Schwer* . . . . Mother takes up her needlework,
frowning into the long silence, staring at the two
broad faces that mirror her husband, our father,
whose nails held red dirt, hands coarse as rope
against her back, bed creaking as he rose at dawn.

STRENGTH

When with one hand Joe Little Bear lifted
the drill collar from his foot
and sighed as if waking from a long sleep,
it is odd how we were weakened by this,
how we all became children watching
our fathers wrestling with our uncles
or hoisting a huge cottonwood log on one shoulder
and smiling down to remind us that we did not yet belong
to the world, that strength lay in the lifting
of things heavier and larger than ourselves.

And thus did we return to the wash room
that day with our black hands and pale shoulders
and turned away from the photographs
of bronze women we knew we could never have.
Later that weekend when we carried Little Bear
again from the tavern holding his blood-caked fists
to his chest like crushed roses
and mumbling the prayers and curses
of another language, then too we felt uneasy,

and on the road to his tar paper shack
something cold fell around us
as we watched the distant fires
of the moon through the branches that passed by overhead.
Little Bear's horse stood waiting in the makeshift corral,
and its head turned so that the one moon-
lit eye came at us like a train in a tunnel of light,
came rushing toward us, beyond strength
or weakness, and Little Bear was singing
and our bodies turned to water and ran slowly out of our lives.

THE LAST DAYS

Out here, where the high wires pitch and whine
and blue stem rakes the tops of my wrists,
the sky seems to worry itself into dusk,
clouds thinning into mares' tails,
a rasp of grackles keening into the west wind,
tumbleweeds that lunge, then hang
on the rusted barbs of hard, angry possession.

Rows of stubble veer toward the poplar trees
that shield my house from blowing top-soil,
and through the branches a lighted window shines:
my son and daughter lost in books,
my wife awash with the colors of the TV screen.
And the pane of glass that comes between us
seems as distant, as final, as the stars.

For hours I have walked the fences
of these separate fields where the dying light
grows long and mottled over bunches
of shorn maize stalks and rotted fenceposts,
where last night's dream comes flashing back
like the sputtering red lights of the town's
last elevator warning off low flights:

My grandmother holds my face between her palms
and pleads, *release the dead, let them rise up*
and walk the bankrupt fields and turn them
back to wilderness, the way we found them.
Let those who died to hold the land be gathered
in the failing town, then let the sun reclaim
the earth, let it burn, oh, let it all come down.

PHOTOGRAPH OF A COLLEGE FOOTBALL TEAM, 1927

> *Ohi ombre vane, fuor che ne l'aspetto!*
> –Purgatorio

Before the shutter closes, before the light has gathered,
the one with Nietzsche eyebrows and granite jaw glances
    to his right
nervously as though drawn to the edge of things, drifting
for the errant long pass, the cruel possibility
that two years of seminary and mental collapse
    will never reveal.

In the back row the broad face of a Navajo
hovers over the landscape of his shoulders.
The tongue of his own language ripples through him
like an explosion of birds from a thicket.
It is morning, the dawn light lying down in a dream of horses.

On his left a hog-nosed boy
grips the ball hard with blunt fingers, hair parted down
    the middle
straight as the furrow behind his father's plow in Salina,
    Kansas.
He is walking away from a white frame house,
a sky half-black with a dust cloud, an absence of trees.

Like auras around their bruised, immaculate bodies,
the reflected lights of the flash seem to cloak them
    in their unlived lives,
the future that looms, diminishing, the long walk
through the coliseum tunnel when the cries have died away
and the rumble of cleats against pavement rolls through
    darkness

louder and louder. The gargantuan center must have slumped
like a broken god when he walked away from defeat,
for here he sits brooding, black hair
drooping into his eyes, still listening into the white silence
between the snap and the clatter of shoulderpads.

But the blonde one seated slightly apart on the front row
is staring straight through the camera. His eyes and
      child's face
remind me of that photograph of Rimbaud where
      the murderous smirk
is just beginning at the corners of the mouth. The electric hair,
the spiny arms and hands, the way the head is tilted back
      just so—

this is the one who *knows*,
and moments before making that long climb toward sleep,
I see him standing quite still in a green field watching
      the black hole
in the center of the ball's perfect spiral, the blurred rim
      of crowd
and stadium, and the huge bodies halting, then falling,
      through the broken air.

THE SOLILOQUY OF THE APPLIANCE REPAIRMAN

They bring me their broken toasters,
chrome-dulled and shorted on lumps of grease,
twisted mixmasters with mangled blades
and bent spindles punch-drunk
and beaten into an early grave.
And I, healer and name-brand magician,
I must raise them from the dead,
prop them up and coax their failed motors
into the life-signs of hum and whir.

They go out, they come back,
these wounded, cracked plastic-and-chrome marvels
of the mediocre, of the watery omelette
and bland, confused marguerita.
We should learn from our mistakes:
the lawnmower plugged with muddy oil
will foul again, and again
the nightmare ice-maker will vomit
its perfectly formed cubes into the void.
Freon again, and oh ever again, freon
spewing through the endless circuitry of the freezer,
thumping along, hissing through leaks.

The two Italian girls who lugged in
the computerized cappuccino machine,
chattering and letting their bright eyes
and flashing hands erase the shadows
of the shop—how could they have known my limits:
the modern and high tech, the microwave ovens,
for instance, with their digital read-outs
and soft little gongs that puzzled me

almost into retirement months ago.
Give it up, my wife said,
you're as obsolete as they are,
pointing to the pre-war junk piling up unclaimed.

The girls frowned and took it back.
Hunching their shoulders like old women,
they stumbled out, letting the door bang shut,
flinging the shop back into darkness.
I have learned from the inventions of history,
but I live in the age of wonders,
of the self-contained and irreparable,
where I stand and watch
the small, good things of my hands
drifting far away into the corners of my life.

SAIPAN

After the war,
the men, the tired men,
turned inside their bodies, turned
away as the light crumbled
over the park benches where they lay
under newspapers and held bottles
like sleeping babies to their chests.

My father would say, *they never
returned, they never quite came back.*
Everywhere, the arms of men
in rolled brown sleeves, tattoo
like a bruise—SEMPER FI,
always faithful—blue heart rippling

as the hand flipped ashes
from a Lucky Strike in the back booth
of a neighborhood bar
or a pool hall where green fields
lay before us like small countries and the arms
moved slowly back and forth behind a gauze of smoke.

At twilight we would see the men in their giant shadows
watering lawns, walking circles within circles
in white undershirts that blazed with the day's last light,
or fishing alone on piers:
the rod delicately held, eyes
reaching across the Pacific to its burnished rim.

I thought they were dead, somehow.
At night resting my head on my father's pillow,
the silk one embroidered with SAIPAN
in flames from a dragon's mouth,
I would think of the dead
and be afraid of their gray eyes and blue arms

and sink into my dreamless sleep
and the long dark fields of nothing.

PART THREE:
THE SYSTEM OF WHICH
THE BODY IS ONE PART

THERE IS CONSTANT MOVEMENT
IN MY HEAD

The choreographer from Nebraska
is listening to her mother's cane
hammering the dance floor, down, down,
like some gaunt, rapacious bird
digging at a rotted limb. The mother
still beats time in her daughter's head.

There is constant movement in my head,
the choreographer begins. In Nebraska
I learned dance and guilt from my mother,
held my hands out straight until the cane
beat my palms blue. I was a wild bird
crashing into walls, calming down

only to dance. When Tallchief came down
from New York, a dream flew into my head:
to be six feet tall, to dance the *Firebird*
all in black and red, to shock Nebraska
with my naked, crazy leaps until the cane
shook in the furious hand of my mother.

Well, that day never came. My mother
thought I could be whittled down,
an oak stump to carve into some cane
she could lean on. But in my head
were the sandhill cranes that crossed Nebraska
each fall: sluggish, great-winged birds

lumbering from our pond, the air bird-
heavy with cries and thrumming. My mother
knew. She said I would leave Nebraska,
that small-town life could only pull me down.
Then her hands flew up around her head
and she hacked at the air with her cane.

There are movements I can't forget: the cane
banging the floor, dancers like huge birds
struggling into flight, and overhead,
the choreography of silver cranes my mother
always watched when the wind blew down
from the sandhills and leaves fell on Nebraska.

This dance is the cane of my mother.
The dancers are birds that will never come down.
They were all in my head when I left Nebraska.

THE DRUNK FOREMAN

The tossed bottle shatters on a derrick boom,
littering the iron-yard. The foreman, shit-
faced and sad with old tunes, hurls curses
at a moonless sky blank as a bald tire.

Silent, he slumps on the pipe rack, watching
the plains in its hard sleep, the way
the earth waits, unwinding the long breath
that outlives men, grinding stone on stone

like the clenched jaw of nightmare. Red clods
and stubble scrape like papers in the wind's gust,
and he bangs the hoist chain on pipe, shouting
down every woman who won't have him. Drunk,

he's deaf to the earth's groan and the scream
behind his eyes when he sees his life pinned
flat across the fields the way the yard light
throws down a jagged shadow of mesquite branch.

One more pint and he's blind, photos of ex-wife
and kids washed pale as bone in his back-pocket.
Dumb and bootless, he tumbles into childhood:
dirt farms and thin-wristed women who sang hymns.

Then sleep. His head drops back, skin on steel.
The ground that rolls beneath his dangling hand
uncovers a sun still there. The men gather with
washcloths, coffee, pleas that sound like prayers.

ANGELS

Elliot Ray Neiderland, home from college
one winter, hauling a load of Herefords
from Hogtown to Guymon with a pint of
Ezra Brooks and a copy of Rilke's *Duineser
Elegien* on the seat behind him, saw the ass-end
of his semi sliding around in the side mirror
as he hit ice and knew he would never live
to see graduation or the castle at Duino.

In the hospital, head wrapped like a gift
(the nurses stuck a bow on top), he said
four flaming angels crouched on the hood, wings
spread so wide he couldn't see, and then
the world collapsed. We smiled and passed a flask
around. Little Bill and I sang *Your Cheatin'
Heart*, and laughed, and then a sudden quiet
put a hard edge on the morning, and we left.

Siehe, ich lebe, Look, I'm alive, he said,
leaping down the hospital steps. The nurses
waved, white dresses puffed out like pigeons
in the morning breeze. We roared off in my Dodge,
Behold, I come like a thief! he shouted to the town
and gave his life to poetry. He lives, now,
in the south of France. His poems arrive
by mail, and we read them and do not understand.

SHEETS

Morning rides its gray horse
over the four-sided gambrel roofs
heavy with new snow,
and I imagine your mother
behind the one lighted window
sewing the hems of sheets, curtains,
clothes for your children,

and thinking of the vacant house
where as children we would spread sheets
over the willow trees in the side yard.
From Mrs. Tate's across the street
they must have looked like giant mushrooms,
a great, slumbering cloth forest
risen suddenly from the hands of children.
And at night, how strange it was,
peeling away a sky of sheets to reveal
another sky with its purple going black,
its cold air and stars rushing in
through the opened branches.

We would walk home
dragging the sheets over our shoulders,
tired and resigned as our fathers coming home from work,
or Greek actors tossing their masks onto the grass,
already considering the burdens
of family, lovers, money. But again,

the next day there we were,
our arms full of folded sheets,
and we would spread them out carefully
and begin to place them over the willow trees.

WORK

Work is a transient form of mechanical energy by means of which certain transformations of other forms of energy are brought about through the agency of a force acting through a distance.... Work done by lifting a body stores mechanical potential energy in the system consisting of the body and the earth. Work done on a body to set it in motion stores mechanical kinetic energy in the system of which the body is one part. —Handbook of Engineering Fundamentals

I. Work

Drill collars lie on racks and howl
in the blunt wind. A winch truck waits
in the shop yard beside an iron block,
hook and cable coiling down, dragging
through dirt that blows in yellow gusts.

East across a field where the slag sky
of morning bends down, a man walks away
from a white frame house and a woman
who shouts and waves from the back porch.
He can hear the shop doors banging open.

Inside, where the gray light lifts dust
in swirls, tools rest like bodies dull
with sleep, lead-heavy. The lathe
starts its dark groan, the chuck's jaw
gripping an iron round, the bit set.

Outside, the man approaches the iron block,
a rotary table, judging its weight,
the jerk and pull on the hoist chain.
A bad sun heaves the shadow of his house
outward. He bends down. A day begins.

II. The Body

Looping the chain through the block's eyes,
he makes a knot and pulls the cable hook through.
The winch motor starts up, reeling in cable slowly
until it tightens, then drops to a lower gear
and begins to lift. The motor's whine brings
machinists to the shop windows, sends sparrows

fluttering from high-wires where the plains wind
gives its thin moan and sigh. When the brake
is thrown, the block jerks and sways five feet

above the earth, straining to return, popping
a loose cable thread and making the gin poles
screech in their sockets like grief-stricken women.

From the house the man is lost in the blaze of a sun
gorged to bursting and mirrored in the shop's
tin side. The block hangs, black in the red air.

III. The Body And The Earth

Beneath the rotary table the man reaches up
to remove the huge bearings, and oil winds
down his arm like a black rope. He places
each bearing big as a pendulum in the sun

where it shines, swathed in grease.
It is the heart of the day, and he feels
the long breeze cool his face and forearms,
wet now with the good sweat of hard work.

The wind scrapes through stubble, making
a papery sound that reminds him of harvest:
him, his father, the field hands crowded around
a beer keg to celebrate the week's cut, dirt

drying to mud on their damp faces, leaving
bruises and black masks. Now, kneeling
in the block's cool shadow, he watches clods
soak up the brown pools of oil and sweat.

IV. The System Of Which The Body Is One Part

On the down side of the work day,
when the wind shifts and heat stuns the ground
like an iron brand, the machinists lean
into the shadow of the shop's eaves
and gulp ice water, watching the yard hand now

as he struggles in his black square
to slip each bearing back in place, each steel ball
that mirrors back his eyes, the stubble field, the shop,
the white frame house, the sun, and everything beyond,
the whole circumference of seen and unseen, the world

stretching away in its one last moment when the chain
makes that odd grunting noise, and sighs *click*, and then *click*,
and sings through the eyes of the block as it slams the ground
and the earth takes the thud and the men freeze
        and the woman strolls out
to see that has happened now in the system of which
        the body is one part.

THE CITY OF GOD

Everything is as it should be.

Water and light, for instance, have not changed.

The beasts of the field refuse to be beautiful.
They harbour enormous secrets. Their boredom is exquisite.

Grief is migratory. Seasonally it is seen flying
in a new direction in its distinctive "V" pattern.

The scene of one's childhood is always there
and never revisited: the garage out back,
    the yellow Studebaker with mud flaps,
the broken water heater, the smell of ammonia.

Someone is always telling a story.

The abandoned shoe on the roadside contains the memory
    of Proust.
The tin siding banging in the wind is the Schubert two-cello
    quintet.

Stars and planets are still stars and planets,
and there is not the remotest chance of ever voyaging to one.

Sleep is optional.

In moments of depression you can go to the back window
    and see wild deer
crossing the lawn. They freeze, sensing your presence,
    and will not move
until you do.

Disasters happen every two or three years and everyone
    survives.

Desire is a dream of blue meadows and chestnut trees.
Fulfillment is the clamor of rain against palm leaves
    as you dream.

Falling occurs, but without a sinking feeling. Rising occurs,
but without the spiritual implications.

Politicians are kites with heavy tails.
Children have given up on them and tossed them idly by.

Your grandfather's ivory dominoes, long misplaced,
are rediscovered daily.

The old library is just the way it used to be, only more so.

Baseball is played all year. The Dodgers have returned
    to Brooklyn.

On summer evenings, the shadows move backward
    into the branches of trees,
leaving behind traces of sound somewhat like Eric Satie
    heard from a distance.

Everything is as it was.
Everything is as it will be.

Imperfection is a mark of divinity. God is praised for his
    lack of talent.

THE WOMAN AT THE LAUNDROMAT
CRYING "MERCY"

And the glass eyes of dryers whirl
on either side, the roar just loud enough
to still the talk of women. Nothing
is said easily here. Below the screams
of two kids skateboarding in the aisles
thuds and rumbles smother everything,
even the woman crying *mercy, mercy.*

Torn slips of paper on a board swear
Jesus is the Lord, nude photo sessions
can help girls who want to learn, the price
for Sunshine Day School is affordable,
astrology can change your life, any
life. Long white rows of washers lead
straight as highways to a change machine

that turns dollars into dimes to keep
the dryers running. When they stop,
the women lift the dry things out and hold
the sheets between them, pressing corners
warm as babies to their breasts. In back,
the change machine has jammed and a woman
beats it with her fists, crying *mercy, mercy.*

DECEMBER, 1986

Dry socket of the solstice,
dull rub of a turning year.
Doors open all across town. Overhead,
new weather spreads like traffic.

Winter dialectic:
the brewery dispenses men and beer each evening,
drinking day away too soon,
taverns crammed with short lives,
long nights.

I'm in Hermann's,
huddling with friends like thieves.
Voices collect in clouds,
laboring-class lives thick,
intricate as snow settling into mounds
of soft syllables, close and not cold.

THE ROBINSON HOTEL

The windows frame a sun in white squares.
  Across the street
the Bluebird Cafe leans into shadow and the cook
  stands in the doorway.
Men from harvest crews step from the Robinson
  in clean white shirts
and new jeans. They stroll beneath the awning,
  smoking Camels,
considering the blue tattoos beneath their sleeves,
  Friday nights
in San Diego years ago, a woman, pink neon lights
  rippling in rain water.
Tonight, chicken-fried steak and coffee alone
  at the Bluebird,
a double feature at The PLAZA: *Country Girl,*
  The Bridges at Toko-Ri.
The town's night-soul, a marquee flashing orange
  bulbs, stuns the windows
of the Robinson. The men will leave as heroes,
  undiscovered.
Their deaths will be significant and beautiful
  as bright aircraft,
sun glancing on silver wings, twisting, settling
  into green seas.
In their rooms at night, they see Grace Kelly
  bending at their bedsides.
They pass their hands slowly across their chests
  and raise their knees
against the sheets. The PLAZA's orange light
  fills the curtains.
Cardboard suitcases lie open, white shirts folded
  like pressed flowers.

PART FOUR:
IN CZECHOSLOVAKIA

IN ANOTHER LIFE I ENCOUNTER MY FATHER

There we are in the same outfield,
a minor league team named after some small
but ferocious animal—the Badgers, say,
or Bulldogs. The town is heavily industrial,
Peoria maybe, and the slap of the fungo bat
keeps us moving over the worn grass—in,
then back, where a blonde drinking a beer
is painted crudely on a white fence.
Big drops of condensation drape the bottle,
which is angled toward her open mouth.
We want to joke about this, but don't.
He is new on the team, and we are uneasy
with each other. When a high one drifts
far to his right, he takes it on a dead run.
He is more graceful than I am, and faster.

In the dugout he offers me a chew,
and we begin to talk—hometown, college ball,
stuff like that. A copy of Rimbaud
sticks out of my pocket, and I give him
the line about *begging the day for mercy.*
He frowns, spitting, working his glove.
We begin to talk politics, baseball
as ideology, more embracing than Marxism.
He seems interested, but something is wrong.
The sky is getting a yellow tinge.
The heavy air droops over my shoulders,
and the locusts begin their harangue.
When I go to the plate, the ball
floats by fat as a cantaloupe, and I
slam it through the left field lights.

I can do no wrong, but we are losing.
The coach, an alcoholic, is beginning
to cry over his second wife. His wails
unnerve us. The catcher is stoned,
and we may have to forfeit. The new guy
is unperturbed and praises me lavishly
on my fine play. In the outfield I point out
Draco and Cassiopeia, almost missing one
that drives me into the fence. I hold
the ball high and tip my cap, the crowd
roars, blood runs down my back. Walking in,
he knows I am playing over my head, but says
nothing. We hear the batboy's shriek,
the coach's tired moan. The locusts
are shredding the air like bandsaws,
the scoreboard is blazing at the edges,
and we know that the game will never end.

L'ATTENTE

The little man sitting at the top of the stairs
looked up at me through eyes dark and unreachable
as stones at the bottom of a pond, and said,
Waiting is the brother of death.

In Degas' painting, a woman dressed
in the native costume of death waits
seated on a bench beside her daughter,
a ballerina in blue ribbons and white
crinoline who is bent over slightly
as if she might be ill, ill with waiting,
the harness of the future heavy
around her neck. The mother leans forward,
elbows resting on thighs, and holds
her umbrella out before her in a kind
of resignation, a dropped semaphore,
a broken code. She is beyond language,
and though you cannot see her eyes
beneath the wide brim of her black hat,
something about the jaw and chin, some
thin line of shadow, tells you the eyes
are set in the dazed stare of memory,
the white gloves she wears are the white dresses
of childhood, the white Sunday mornings
narrowing toward the vanishing point
like rows of sycamore along the boulevard.

I said to the little man at the top
of the stairs, *Yes, I know, I am waiting, too.*
And I invited him in for a cup of tea.
Then we sat down at the table on the balcony
drinking our tea, not speaking, warm
in each other's company, like children
waiting for a ballet class to begin,
waiting for the dancing to begin.

CHILD AND DWARF

> *ah, but my heart, my bent-over blood,*
> *all the distortions that hurt me inside*
> —Rilke, "The Dwarf's Song"

Knees under chin beneath a turmoil
of Rodin's struggling torsos, a child
watches a woman smaller than a child

striding through the museum foyer.
The tall bronze doors sigh shut.
The woman pauses, then begins circling

the Rodin, stricken by a cylinder
of light breaking through the atrium.
The child's eyes pursue the woman

like a lover's, and a thin smile
curls to lift and draw her slowly
through the widening pool of light.

Now the gnarled fingers of a figure's
outstretched hand hold them there,
blond hair twisting down their spines,

arms almost touching, girl and woman
watching three men wrestling, it seems,
to escape the prison of their skins.

Dwarf and child turn, then, to see,
eye to eye, the child that isn't,
the child that is, the distortions

of the body, mind, and eye, and
with the shifting light, the sculpture
seems to move beneath a mass of shadows,

the too large heads stretching the tendons
of the neck, the long arms lengthening,
the great hands grasping in the coiling air.

LOCAL KNOWLEDGE

It seems hard to find an acceptable answer to the question of how or why the world conceives a desire, and discovers an ability, to see itself, and appears to suffer the process. That it does so is sometimes called the original mystery.
—G. Spencer Brown, *Laws of Form*

I.

A rusted-out Ford Fairlane with red star hubcaps
skids up to Neiderland Rig Local No. 1
heaving Travis Deeds into a swirl of dust
and rainbowed pools of oil and yellow mud.

> *Dear Father,*
>   *As you can see I have*
> *come pretty far north with this bunch*
> *almost to Dodge city in a stretch*
> *of wheat field flat and blowed out as any*

Rows of drill collars stand in racks and howl
in the blunt wind. Chain and hoist cable
bang the side of a tin bunkhouse as men
with hangovers wake to the drum of a new day.

> *to be seen in West Texas. All things*
> *are full of weariness, as the man says,*
> *and I am one of those things, dog-tired*
> *and not fit to shoot. I am glad*

Crowding around the rig floor where the long
column of iron reaches straight down through rock
and salt water, Travis and the men grab
the big tongs and throw them on, then off,

to hear you are back with your church
in Odessa if that is what you want
and if that old bottle does not bring
you down again though it is a comfort

hauling up one length of pipe, then another
as the bit drags out of the hole, coming up
with crushed rock and shark's teeth from old strata
once under ocean. The drawworks lurches, rumbling

to me, which you do not want to hear,
but alone up there in the crow's nest
with the wind screaming at me
and that old devil moon staring down

loud enough to smother talk, and the men
work under the iron brand of the noon sun
until mud covers them. Their arms and faces
blacken, and gas fumes sting their eyes.

and nothing all around, you get to thinking
you are pretty much nothing yourself.
But I am all O.K., staying out
of trouble, and I do not know where

Two hundred feet up, the crown block pulleys
wail on their axles like high wires, keening.
Travis leans back to see the black mud hose curl
into a question mark looming from earth to sun.

I am going in this world but am looking
as always for a fat paycheck and then
I will be home again. Take good care
of yourself.
> *Your loving son,*
> *Travis*

II.

Travis Deeds' tongue, throat, wide mouth:
singers of broken tunes and his father's hymns
in dry creek beds alone with Jack Daniels
and the arc of night, the revolving stars.

> *Dearest son,*
> What gain has the worker
> from his toil? *I'm a little short here,*
> *and if you could spare maybe fifty?*
> *Am back on my feet, though, feisty*

The eyes pink from booze, dust, and sunlight,
sleepless beneath a football scar that slices
the left eyebrow like a scythe, readers
of *Job* and *Ecclesiastes*, crazed in moonlight.

> *and full of the Word.* So I turned
> to consider wisdom and madness
> and folly, *and so should you for one*
> *of these days God will show His face*

Belly, back, shoulders pale as eggs,
once-broken arm bent slightly, hands mottled
with scraped knuckles and blue fingernails
that thrum like drumfish with the blood's pulse.

> *to you as He has to me, you think*
> *your alone in the world, that your*
> *nothing, but you are not, believe me.*
> *There is more to life than sweat*

Birthmark like a splash of acid on one thigh,
darkening hair of the loins, sad cock, legs thick
as stumps, knees yellow-brown with old bruises,
ludicrous feet, small toes curled like snails.

and dirt and oil and fat paychecks.
Remember, better is a handful
of quietness than two hands full
of toil and a striving after wind.

Slowly the traveling block lifts his body
to the rig's top. Blonde hair blazing, he sings
flat against the hard wind, rising, staring down
into the rig's black strata, the fossil kingdom.

> *I know this in my poor banged-up soul.*
> *I hope you can come home soon,*
> *for it is lonely as hell here.*
>
> > *Love,*
> > *Avon*

III.

Gargantuan plates move over the mantle of the earth.
The jammed crust up-thrusts and rivers spill down,
dumping red dirt in layers, choking themselves dry.
On the west, the Pecos River; on the east,

> *Dear Father,*
> *Enclosed is a check*
> *for fifty bucks, please hang onto it.*
> *Good news here. The geologist took*
> *what is called a core sample and says*

canyons of the high plains: Palo Duro,
Tule, Casa Blanca, Quitaque, Yellow House.
Calcium bubbles up to form the caprock.
Sod grass spreads under the wind. The dirt holds.

> *that it is a sure thing this time.*
> *As for your letter, you say not*
> *to feel like nothing, but I found out*
> *there is alot to be said for nothing.*

Around the rig now, plowed fields lose the dirt
in gusts, and roughnecks breathe through rags
like small-time bandits. Five miles east, a gray wolf
leaves its kill beneath a jagged branch of mesquite.

> *The other night I was alone*
> *with just the moon and the stars*
> *and the locusts buzzing away*
> *and could look down the hole*

Under the raucous sky sandhill cranes ruffle
the pond water with their wings, lumbering into flight.
Everywhere the flat land has given up its wheat
and maize, and dust rises along the horizon

> *into the nothing of the earth*
> *and above into the nothing of the sky*
> *and there I was in the middle*
> *of it all until I was nothing too*

like a huge planet out of orbit, colliding.
Travis Deeds, greasing the crown block,
leans against the wind and sees the open mouth
of the sun slowly drowning in the brown air.

> *not even Travis Deeds but just the eye*
> *that the world uses to look at itself.*
> *So maybe that is a place in the world,*
> *not that you would agree. But I am*

IV.

Crew, drawworks, the whole rig floor are dragged
under the dirt-floor, roughneck shouts sinking
beneath the wind's harangue, the berserk clatter
of chains, cable, bunkhouse roof yanking loose.

on day shift now and if the geologist
is right and we are right next door
to pay dirt, I should be home soon
with my sack full.
                    Your loving son,
                            Travis

And for a while in the sudden rush and whirl
the body clings to the crown block, grease-slick
hands grasping, then spilling like fish over
the iron rails as the false night swallows

Dearest son,
        Received the fifty
which I accept with the blessings
of God as a small tithing but
at a dear cost what with that raving

the land the way the land folds its creatures
into bed-rock fossils. The body is blown free.
The arms wheel, the legs blunder like tossed sticks,
the soft earth surrounds and pulls him down.

about the eye of the world and such
crazy talk. A man is more than
just the world—sky, earth, stone, tree.
Yes, I know, from dust to dust,

Blood batters the heart in flight, pounding
like the flailing wings of cranes, the quickening
breath of the wolf returning to his kill,
the mesquite branch shaking in the nervous wind.

but in between, he is something, a man
above and against the world, and so
he builds dams and lays down roads
and draws oil out of hard rock

Put forth thy hand now and touch his bone and flesh.
And the men gather where he slams the ground,
where the body is the obedient son of gravity,
where the hands claw the thickening dust, where

> *just like you are doing now. The world*
> *can only bring him down but God*
> *will pull him up like He did for that*
> *good man Job. Come home quick.*
> > *Love,*
> > *Avon*

the buckled spine rages, where the unknowable God
does not speak the unknowable answer and the great wing
folds and unfolds and once more under the sun's
long pull the wind makes its hollow yowl of lament.

MY MOTHER'S DREAMS

Huddled with your trembling sisters
under pounds of patchwork quilts the night
Black Bear Creek spilled over the Oto,
you dreamed green meadows, white fences,
and sloe-eyed, smiling cows that never
needed milking. In Oak City, selling
shoes to Ginger Rogers, you drank nickel
beer after work, elbow to silk elbow
with a good-looking blonde later known
as Pretty Boy Floyd. Your dreams hooted
like depression trains, you said, hobos
leaping into ditches, then springing up
like cartoon bears to croon lullabies
the way the Andrews Sisters sang *Argentine
Nights*. And rushing through the tunnel
of the war's long night, the usual Freudian
mob of spiders, floating fish, and falling
teeth must have raised you up to sit, alone,
beneath a single light where you browsed
through photographs of my father, tan and
shirtless, on an island like the island
from the week before. *My own flesh and
blood*, you said, when my grandmother died,
and I wondered if you dreamed that way,
violence as metaphor for the ways we live
and die. On V-Day in San Jose you woke
to dirigibles and apricots, Chagall's
green sky. Over oranges and coffee
you told your friend the dream of flowers
within flowers, red petals falling away
to a cobble street where couples strolled
through waves of sunlight and smiled and
smiled again,

and later, one night after
making love, you dream a dense, slow dream
of caves, paths, streams leading to a road
that winds forever, and there, the white
rabbit behind the dark hedge, there I am,
and in the morning over breakfast, you say
to my father, *I had the strangest dream,*
and you go on in that loose meander
of dream talk, and he almost listens,
humming, feeling the sun's slow touch,
idly stroking the perfect rim of his cup.

THE MARCH OF THE SUICIDES

Wherever they move,
the earth crumbles beneath them
and the glass wings of cicadas are raised against the stars.

Like women washing on river banks,
some of them kneel and press their palms into the ground,
the lustrations of those who have abandoned the earth.

Pinned on their garments are notes
like those found on school children
whose mothers frown and bend down to read their chests.

Their cries at sunrise are not frightening.
Infants wake to see them swooning into their own shadows,
the bronze shadows over ponds in winter.

Their hands are blue
and their dusty eyes revolve constantly
like moons unmoored from ocean, tree, and stone.

Memory accompanies them everywhere,
an ill-fitting cloak
that makes their shoulders seem luminescent and heavy.

Often, passing beneath mulberry trees
or window ledges, they croon a one-note song,
the sound of a steel ball spinning, perfectly honed.

They will call you only once,
as you sit there in the half-light
and cannot see the ends of your arms.

IN CZECHOSLOVAKIA

It is 1968, and you are watching a movie
called *The Shop on Main Street,* about a man—
an ordinary man, a carpenter—in Czechoslovakia,
who is appointed Aryan Controller of a poor button shop
belonging to the widow Lautman, who is old
and deaf and has the eyes of a feverish child.
She smiles in luminous gratitude for almost anything—
the empty button boxes, a photo of her lost daughters,
the man, Tono, who she believes has come to help her.

At the point where the two meet—she, kind but confused,
he, awkward and somewhat ashamed—you notice a woman
in the front row who keeps bending toward the seat
beside her and whispering and letting her hand drift
lovingly toward whomever—a child, you suppose—is there.
The woman's frizzy hair catches the reflected light
from the screen, a nimbus of fire around her head
as she turns to share her popcorn with the child whose
fine blonde hair and green eyes you have begun to imagine.

In the movie Tono has failed to explain his position
to the widow and is acting as her helper in exchange
for monthly payments from the Jewish community.
He is contented, his ambitious wife is enjoying
dreams of prosperity and a heightened sexuality,
it is that terrible time when everyone is happier
than they should be, and then of course the trucks
move in, the dependable gray trucks that have made
life somewhat impossible in the twentieth century.

Now the woman in the front row has returned
to her seat and is handing a Coke to the child
hidden by the chair back, then reaching over
with a handkerchief to wipe the child's mouth
and smile and whisper out of that explosion of hair

she wears. The widow Lautman cannot understand
the trucks or Tono's dilemma that either she must go
or he will be arrested as a collaborator, and as he
stands there pleading, going crazy in her husband's suit

which she has given to him, her eyes widen
like opened fists and she knows now and begins
to shout, *pogrom, pogrom,* with her hands trembling
like moths around her face, and when he panics and
hurls her into the closet to hide her, she falls
and oh Jesus he has killed her and he cries out,
I am a zero, but you think, *no, no, it's worse,
you're a man,* and now the woman in the front row
is shouting at the child, it's misbehaved in some way,

and when you look up my God Tono has hung himself
in the suit that belonged to the widow's husband,
the suit he was married in, and then, miraculously,
Tono and the widow are floating arm in arm,
smiling, dancing out into the sun-drenched boulevard,
dancing away from you and history, resurrected
into the world as it might be but somehow cannot be,
a grove of light where the cobbled streets and trees
with their wire skirts are glossy after a soft rain

and the world deepens without darkening and the faces
of everyone are a kind of ovation, and then it's over,
you think, the house lights go up, and you're sitting there
stunned and the woman from the front row walks out
into the aisle with her hand out behind her as if gripping
another, smaller hand. And you see it, though
you don't want to, because you are a man or a woman,
you see that there is nothing there, no child,
nothing, and the woman stops and bends down to speak

to the child that isn't there and she has this smile
of adoration, this lacemaker's gaze of contentment,
she is perfectly happy, and she walks on out
into the street where people are walking up and down
and where you will have to walk up and down
as if you were on a boulevard in Czechoslovakia
watching the gray trucks rumble by like a chain
of circus animals as you go on thinking and
breathing as usual, wreathed in your own human skin.

DUST STORM

The churning wind thickened to a brown pond,
a clod, grit between my teeth, lungs sucking
clotted air like wings beating on a dirt bank.

It filled the shop, and the windows above
the lathes sank under a ton of dust that coiled
where chinks in the tin roof sent down shafts

of light. The bookkeeper raged and slapped the panes
of his glass cage, his shouts vague as fog.
We could not see our hands in front of our eyes

when the foreman slid the big front door shut
in the dark, the sullen, rank dark that washed
over us as we pressed red rags to our faces.

For hours we lay on the wooden platforms
beside our lathes or stumbled toward
the shop's center and huddled there like thieves

before an open fire, the night-dust sifting
around us until we were old men with gray hair,
and black creases across our foreheads.

When the windows began yellowing
and the floor paled and our hands came floating
back from the pond bottom, the foreman

dragged the huge door slowly open, and this
is what still comes in my dreams: the glacier
of light that moved down from the horizon,

came lunging into the great cave of the shop,
that iron light rumbling toward us,
grinding and shattering the stale air,

a world of light, a sun bludgeoning our eyes,
blinding the town laden with dirt behind us,
and beneath that flaming square, the men

in their little silhouettes, like children pulled
from the smothering earth, the blind, burnt
figures of children who raised their hands

in joy and terror and flashed their eyes
beneath layers of dust, coming into the light
as it moved down and embraced them and took them up.

AFTERWORD: LATHEWORK

As a child in west Texas, I am standing beside my father as he works a machine lathe at a shop in one of several dusty oilfield towns, usually boom towns, that we would move through. As a boy in the small town of Liberal, Kansas, I am standing in front of the old library on the corner of Third Street and Kansas Avenue reading Ernest Thompson Seton's *Biography of a Grizzly*. As a young man I am sitting in a movie theatre witnessing the scene of the mother and child described in the poem, "In Czechoslovakia." I will never forget these particular scenes. Standing in a grocery line, running on a quarter-mile track, watching my son play a Little League game, waiting for a stoplight to change, I will find myself turning one of these images over again in my mind and knowing that this is why I write poems.

The first image, I was to discover, holds the model for everything I have written, especially poems: lathework. In machine shops in Houston, Lubbock, Midland, and Snyder, Texas, I would as a boy stand on the wooden ramp next to my father and watch his hands move gracefully and efficiently over the lathe, maneuvering the levers and rotary handles and making the bit move in and out, back and forth, as the huge chuck spun a section of drill pipe in its iron grip. Once he had the bit set just right, having measured the cut with the calipers, he would let go, and a steady spiral of blue steel shaving would coil out into the darkness, dropping with a hiss into the milky mixture of oil and water below. He would then lean back, light a cigarette, pour himself a cup of coffee, and breathe slowly in that easy, contented way of someone sure of his craft, pleased with his own expertise, confident that the thing was going well, that it was going to be a precise, skillful piece of work.

Almost no words would pass between us. There were only the rumble and occasional whine of the lathe, the damp whisper of the shavings, and the surrounding darkness of the immense cathedral of the shop. That, and the mingled odors of oil and water and sweat and khaki, for my father always wore, like a uniform, a starched khaki workshirt and trousers and a pair of Boss Walloper gloves. But there was no talk, no words.

I wanted to talk, wanted to trouble him out of the mystery of his pure world of work with a small boy's foolish questions, but the same instinct that kept me quiet in church each Sunday kept me quiet now. There were the machinist and the silence and the constant lesson, repeated with each drill collar, each cut of the bit, of a small thing done well.

Things and words. The words came early and in different ways: whole days spent in bed with bronchitis while words floated disembodied from radio dramas in another room where my mother was ironing, late nights at family reunions when booze had loosened the tongues of my usually silent father and his brothers so that they began to tell the stories about growing up in Oklahoma that I never tired of hearing, afternoons with my father at oil rigs where I would listen to the roughnecks cursing each other in that wonderfully inventive way that seemed to make an art of swearing. But words as a world, a separate reality as pure and hermetically enclosed as the world of lathework, did not open to me until one day on a street corner in Liberal, Kansas. We had just moved there from west Texas, and my parents had gone into the bank across the street to open a checking account, leaving me to amuse myself in the town's tiny storefront library. I browsed around, amazed to learn from the ancient one behind the desk *that I was permitted to take books home,* as many as four at a time. I checked out *Biography of a Grizzly,* stepped outside, and leaned against the stoplight completely absorbed in the book and oblivious to the swirl of traffic and people around me. I cannot forget the exhilaration I felt at the time, the centripetal pull of the words, the feeling that I was at the center of something, that between myself and the words on the page was a world bearing significance and authenticity, a world that somehow existed not outside but within the other one.

Growing up in that little town in the heart of the dust bowl, I do not know how I could have survived without the words of the printed page, of books. I wish that I could rhapsodize about the natural beauties of the place, the rich and varied landscape, but I cannot. It was rather bleak, surrounded by wheat and maize fields, with few trees. I recall being out on oil rigs on various jobs, looking out across the barren country treeless from horizon to horizon, listening to the chains beating against the derrick in the ceaseless wind, and waiting, waiting for life to come to some kind of *point*. But it only seemed to come to a point on the printed page, and so I lived, when I could, among books, and words filled up the empty horizon and made for me a necessary world.

Later, as a young man I happened to be sitting alone in a movie theater waiting for the darkness, like sleep, to descend (movies were so like dreams to me), and I noticed several rows in front a woman speaking to someone hidden in the seat beside her. The someone was apparently her child, for she doted on it, smiling expressively, occasionally laughing, talking to it, reaching over to smooth its dress or collar. She even went to the concession stand and brought back a box of popcorn for it. After the movie started, this constant yet unobtrusive stream of maternal affection continued, and when the movie ended, I waited to see what the child looked like. The mother rose and walked out with her hand outstretched as if the child hidden behind the row of seats were following at arm's length, but when they reached the aisle, the mother's hand was holding nothing at all. There was no child. And the woman walked up the aisle and out of the theatre with her hand held out to nothing, occasionally looking down and speaking to the child she only imagined.

To this day I cannot quite explain why that scene will not leave me. Surely there are terror and mystery in it, and perhaps, ignorant of and untouched by the human experience behind the scene, I can afford to be fascinated by it. Perhaps the woman and her imagined child represent for me the unspeakable outer limits of human tragedy, or some arctic zone of the imagination where reality is no longer surpassed but cruelly and impossibly replaced. I think, though, that it is the fact of absence in the scene that will not let me forget it: the absence beneath the mother's hand as she walked out of the theater, the absence of apparent meaning, the absence of a real rather than an imagined life, absences like so many lighted windows as you walk through a strange city, wanting to fill them with imaginary lives and words and stories.

And so, driving past the abandoned basketball court or the small, slowly dying farmtown in Kansas, or sitting before the blank screen after the audience has filed out, I am worried—inspired is certainly not the right word—into the interesting struggle called writing: slow, halting gestures toward that centripetal universe at whose center I stood as a boy on Kansas Avenue. I think now of that struggle as it occurred many years later about four o'clock in the morning in a darkened room, darkened because my two-year old son was sleeping fitfully nearby. There was some trouble in my life, and it seemed to be echoed in the growls of a pack of dogs that passed beneath the window regularly at that time as they roamed the neighborhood overturning trashcans in search of scraps. I was trying to write a poem about my father, a poem I had struggled to write many times before about lathework and the machine shop and the peculiar beauty of blue steel shavings under lamplight. But then, as now, it had no ending, no place to go. And then the dogs moved on and there was only the silence, and I found myself writing, *let words be steel, let them make fine, thin lines across an empty page.* It was a beginning, I thought, I am almost home. I could hear my son's easy breathing in the next room, the slow grind of the lathe, the sigh of the shavings as they dropped into the oil and water below.

for Rafil

JUDITH KROLL

Our Elephant
& That Child

Our works may die, while we live on,
changed by the fact of having created.
–Woman's Mysteries, M. Esther Harding,

JUDITH KROLL. was born in Brooklyn, New York. After attendir Smith College and Yale University, she taught at Vassar Colleg In 1975, she went to India with her husband, a native of New Delh and for the next ten years lived in India. During this time her s Rafil was born. She also began working on translations from t Kannada—poems by 12th-century South Indian mystics. In 1989, s began teaching in the creative writing division of the University Texas at Austin, where she is also affiliated with the Center f Asian Studies. She is the author of *In the Temperate Zone: Poe* (Scribners) and *Chapters in a Mythology: The Poetry of Syl Plath* (Harper & Row).

CONTENTS

I. ARGUMENTS

Thinking About History	8
Freedom	9
Betrayals	11
The Speed of Light	13
On the Street of the Dream	14
First Rumors	15
Figures of Silence	16

II. HILL STATION

At Seven Thousand Feet	18
Dying in the Mountains	20
Hotel Metropole	21
Hill Station	25
Climacteric	26
A View of the Snows	29
Anniversary	31
Late Notes	32
From the Plains	33
Our Elephant	36
Another Ending	39

III. AFTER THE SNOWFALL

After the Snowfall	41
Loving Someone Else	42
ReEntry	42
You Made Me Love You	45
Impossible Choices	46
Kali Yuga	48
"When Everything You Do Is a Mirror"	49
Pronouns	50

Divorce, Etc.   53
How It Is Now   55
The Dream of Elizabeth Hartley   57

IV. THAT CHILD

Winter Birth   64
Ventriloquist   65
Old Light   66
That Child   68

AFTERWORD   71

ARGUMENTS

THINKING ABOUT HISTORY

for John Broomfield

If "Fire is sunlight unwinding from the log,"
what does that tell us of transformations?

Can it explain how this dead white bird
is only a piece of tattered cotton?

I loved to hear the tale of your mother
reading your mind,
reading you into the man
who turns, peering back through the keyhole.

Think how notions are planted—
extermination of weeds,
vermin, people.

So we weave and unwind in a lustrous mosaic,
tapestries lining the cave
where we are, for a time, a spirit possessed by story.

And there, in the luminous field,
the tiniest violet is perfectly rendered;
in every glowing flower

the unicorn sits on folded limbs,
waiting to be real.

FREEDOM

In his blue socks and brown shoes,
the killer is helpless.

The degraded beige of his hair
beneath which his eyes

freight pain like terrified heroes
is helpless.

There is the clock again, ticking.
There is food to be eaten—

bruised apples, the tin of pale beans,
a watery steak gagged in plastic.

Today the woman named I
has been happy.

One fine poem escaped from her this morning,
a stringless kite let loose from the roof of this building

where crushed beer-cans and black dogs
glint in the fire of the sun helplessly shining,

the wet scents of approaching summer
luring her outside.

Shaved and strong, her helpless legs
carry her to the fenced-in park at the corner.

The litter at rest in the street
flares up with a shout,

a chorus of freaks,
and brutal, crutchless joy invades her lungs.

As she kneels to smile back at the yellow pansies
hanging like paper flames,

she is helpless.
The bullet is helpless.

BETRAYALS

Your father dies,
husband in love with your friend,
lover turns away.

And yet what they were, they were
when you freely offered yourself to their radiant mirrors.

What is history
if the fall from an actor's grace
rewrites the past?

Can betrayal too be revised years later? By love?
Love not for you—you have already entered your death—

but love for a woman
with a name you never heard of, a story
you never imagined,
whom you might have gathered to your heart?

So they instruct us: *forgive,*
because we never do know when our acts stop unfolding.
How can we?—the eye of the camera
dilates, flowering irreversibly, to show
how the smallest image contains the world.

And when we assure ourselves "Now I am loving and true,"
then we deliver the wound without our own knowledge.

Or when we betray ourselves—when revenge is worth it—
and we fashion a lie
deliberately to injure the one who turned from us coldly

having made us bloom, seducing us to worship
that marvellous reflection of ourselves—

our lie may do him service in the end.

Is it fearful to conceive this?
Does it strain imagination that this might be so?

Or this: you inform your successor, the woman
at whose insistence he severed you completely:

"While making love to me, he told your secret—
the one he swore never to tell:

your grandfather crossing the sunlit floor of your room,
you at the desk doing schoolwork,

Little one (stroking your hair) *he whispers,*
I want to make you feel good."

Yet how could such exposure fail to help him,
although it may corrupt her mind like a cancer?

And where will it lead you, the agent?

For even if, as you intend, their bond loosens,
will this not exalt him in the end

in that realm where happiness is not a circumstance,
but has only to do with truth?

To live in the fullness of who he truly is—
in the glare of his actions, whatever the cost!

Perhaps in his stillness—beyond desires,
despite himself, he waited for this—

counting on you
one day to call him to account.

THE SPEED OF LIGHT

sometime, someone is writing of this

her hair good brown, she looks out a train window
and notices again how it frames an etching

the innocent greens of the fields
and the dark farmer
in his eye-white headcloth and loincloth, under the sky

and what becomes of our friends?
they blow by us like leaves

as we move in life
into the past and the future

we decide where to send our parents to school
we wake up younger than our children

ON THE STREET OF THE DREAM

The light snapped on at three in the morning.

Who had been going to knock at my door?
How will I ever discover?

Now I swim in a palette of autumn colors—
ochres, oranges, browns,

long shadows falling like pangs
over the road that winds up the mountain.

What was about to pass when the light came on—
was it impending loss,
was it acceptance?

Sometimes that delusion shines so clear:
an intricate memory of something that never happened,

yet look how it's changed you—look at your features, your life.

Can you believe you were never actually there?
(look how you live, without seeing the back of your body)

look in that musty grove with children's voices
roosting in darkening trees where hang,

burning with hope, their future corpses,
not one prepared to believe she is forty—

still she quickens to her girlhood body
crawling on incensed mulch through the hemlock tunnel

her mother told her and told her never to enter.

FIRST RUMORS

Women and men bid quiet farewells
in some fortunate place. The hills of New England?

Women weeping and strong, pioneer women
performing hard work along with their sorrows.

Some are leaving, some will be left behind.
I am both

a tall mother departing the homestead,
the girl trailing her wistfully out to the highway

behind the shepherding men, dry-eyed and stern,
who forbid my looking back.

But the desolate face of that girl
flames in my mind,

it swings
through the scene that opens before me,

the herd breasting a hedge
to a clear view of the highway—

green, billowy trees bent over
a river of concrete,

pale
as a child buried in snow,

and empty cars shoot by like bullets
speeding unstoppably into the vanishing present.

FIGURES OF SILENCE

In Sanskrit the letters are "Little Goddesses."
God and his names are one.
The name will take you across.

Meanwhile, the little helpers—
scene, sound,
woman, man,

I wait till it happens again:
you come in another form,
another disguise, and then

I open the door to a magic cottage
and enter a state of such silence

that all I say is true

and all you answer, the bridge
beneath which I am flowing.

HILL STATION

In such an adventure, the meaning of everything changes.
—Miguel Serrano, *The Serpent of Paradise*

AT SEVEN THOUSAND FEET
(Simla, India)

Every day it is a little nearer,

that huge white wave—the Himalayas
riding the horizon, an army of mountains

that looks much closer than a hundred miles.
Over those ice peaks lies Tibet.
Who knows what is happening there?

It snows in those mountains at night and the whiteness
    advances,
closer each morning—the spreading edge of a sea,

glaciers more etched, and their sharp border
honing itself on the sky.

And over here
the garden withdraws.

Dead twigs, dead roots, leaves yellow and sick.
The flowers one by one giving up,

the thinness of grass pressed to the skull of the earth,
its scalp showing through with a sickly color.

Everywhere piles of litter burning,
the heaped-up rubble

exposing what lies beneath.
Was it always so simple as this—
these few strong lines that tell the whole story?

And again in the morning the mute ranges nearer,
the stuffed-up feeling, a kind of hysteria.

How safe it was in the heat of the summer—
the greenery, the scents, the feverish dreams.

But the flayings of winter get us down to things:
outlines of rocks, outlines of trees.
Does the snow, when it comes, erase or imprison these?

What do I fear, what am I resisting?

The raked-out gardens, the snows encroaching.

DYING IN THE MOUNTAINS

for Ranjan Roy and Arvind Chopra

Silver oaks,
ghosts in an ocean of mist—

the rasp
of the crow's voice

hawk   hawk   hawk
gliding beneath

blue glass, blue sky,
illumination blue of ancient manuscripts,

one small vial a fortune in itself,
and the sun blinding and bright as the primal diamond,

the stone in her ring, the wishless universe
who has waited to marry nothingness for years—

and now her memory is faded like breath,
it is all sweet blankness and effortless rest.

She has learned every lesson from her long engagement.
Everything is difficult before it is easy.

HOTEL METROPOLE

for Zarine

I hadn't really thought of what it means—

the red-tiled roof, the porch arcades,
the smooth lawns hedged with bougainvillea.

I used to ride by it in the clean bright South,

the place I enter in a dream
where the air is a substance altering the body.

What is the name of this feeling? That prince's party—

luncheon for fifty, his stable of antique cars,
the uniformed band squawking jazz like an old record
from a curtained alcove just off the tented room.

The walk to his house through the piney forest
in old jewelry and brilliant silks,
stepping our way among stones and pieces of light.

At the edge of the lawn—three white couches
immaculate, empty, against a backdrop of mountains.

At this hotel we have circled the perfect lawn,
graceful and slow in our heavy saris.

You look like my mother before I was born.

You speak of the terrors of labor,
how it kinked your spine
and for eighteen years the trouble has slowly ascended.

Have we met here before and walked in this garden?
In antique saris and lace blouses
perfectly tailored, the seams like sewn incisions.

Long strands of pearls, eardrops of diamond flowers,
petticoats of satiny percale
brushing cool touches along our thighs.

Under the shade of a carnival-striped umbrella,
we sit in cane chairs the color of ivory.

Outside our circle of shade, the heat
is slowly pressing its pattern into the day.

Look up at the underside of our umbrella,

how the light tries to force its way through—
glowing and threatening, but the canvas holds it.

Around us, bearers in gold-edged turbans
pass with trays of iced lemonade.

Now you are speaking of your long-dead mother,
her famous beauty, her elegant style.
I love to hear of her magic life—

her séances, how men admired her.
Your tall father, noble and brutal.
The breakdowns, the nurses, how you helped her die.

You open a little locket and show me her picture.
A Spanish lady in a black mantilla?
Or maybe a nun with a tragic story—

dawn of the wedding day, everything ready,
then the sudden message: *lost at sea.*

We slip off our sandals and soothe our feet on the grass.
Your slim hands gesture, flashing eight rings.
Are those jewels or bones that live on your fingers?

You gaze at the trellised veranda, its bougainvillea
cascading magenta, the color you love.

Then you turn to me and I see through your eyes,
far down into the speckled amber.

Who are you, then, if not my mother?

Are you about to describe the trials of your marriage?
Am I about to confide my fear of children?

The day around us stills into a painting.
If we move, we move off
into another dream.

Why haven't I asked—am I your sister, your daughter?
Don't tell me yet, let us watch the moment unwind,

the clock-flower dying, its Fabergé body
brief and unworldly, the passion-flower.

Now tell me the name of those lacy trees,
that flower whose color weighs on the eyes.

A tendril of hair escapes and circles your earring.
You sip from a tulip glass in your slender fingers.

"Have you heard," you begin, "the terrible rumor..."

I touch my hair, the moment subsides.
Over there the sunlight falls into the hedges.

I know you love me, also, in some way.

Your nose is a little shiny—it's almost noon.
Let's go and rest on the bed in that cool dark room.
Who do we wait for—is it our husbands, our fathers?

You started to say something once—I shied away
as if I were listening in on a strange conversation.

Now you'll never tell me what it was.

You shade your glass with your palm, a little oasis,
your rings glowing with deep impendingness.

"Let's go in," you say. Have I made a blunder?
I cannot tell if you're pleased or angry.
You rise and move off like a moment of history.

Listen, I tell you in my mind.
Closing a moment like this is not important.
Don't you remember the shape of a circle?

Wait, wait—don't you also feel it?
That trembling on the edge of calm.

HILL STATION

Maybe you should, after all, stay put in this numbing beauty—
you make it the only strength that you need,
and you steal the illusion of peace from these snowy mountains
that ring the horizon, scored by dark clefts,
deep wild feelings tamed by distances.

And the fern-drenched silvery oaks, like wet black legs
plunging down hillsides, past pines breathing mists, and the crows
flinging from tree to tree, and the blackfaced monkeys
eat passion-flowers, perfect and safe, that die for nothing.

It does seem an earthquake, the thought of your leaving this place—
your way of simply putting up with life,
and your stance is the stance of a bear in the mountains:
if something comes to you, you do it.

I'm sorry, maybe I shouldn't probe.
I hate to nudge your monumental calm—
you look so settled inside your glacier.

Is this what you fear—that all waking is waking to pain?
That maybe it's like endless healing, like breaching the
              anesthetic?

Maybe it will hurt too much
if you just start living?

CLIMACTERIC

(*Z. at 49*)

A critical period in life, or a period in which some great change is supposed to take place in the human constitution; especially the so-called change of life or menopause. The climacteric years or critical periods have been supposed to be the years ending the third, fifth, seventh, and ninth period of seven years.... It has been believed that each of these periods is attended with some remarkable change in respect to health, life, or fortune.—Century Dictionary and Cyclopedia

Reclining on a bank of mirrored pillows,
your head tilted back, a sibyl in orange and purple,

the deep silver lids drawn over your eyes,

you bask in your anger, a mad pike
guarding the lightless depths of a crazy river.

Last night, you laughed
in another part of the forest,

hugging and cradling a large pale stone in your lap.
I got it from those ghostly sulphur springs,

pristine, glistening, with the wild green river
rushing between its banks of eggy rocks.

I'm a mad she-ape, and this is my petrified baby.
This one won't leave me, he'll never grow up.

Could you really have said it, with your scorn for dreams
and the smothering love for your late-born son?

All your life you have been a beauty,
each thread in place, a silk magnolia.

The hours you have spent tending the flower of yourself!

But now your eyes flash, luckless gems
trapped in their settings of kohl,

because your tides come dimmer and fewer,
stay longer out—and the bare shores rage.

Soon they'll stay out for good, and you'll be a drift-thing.
A stone or a stick: a dry old woman.

You still haven't made your peace with the moon.

Where is the graceful curving to decline
like the one that men are blessed with?

Why hot news flashes, cruel ransom notes
sent over and over, when the baby's already dead?

So you cling to your late-born son, a familiar
who loves you completely, little ten-year-old mirror.
You've made quite sure of that.

He wears a sullen face like yours,
curved into your body where you lie on your couch,

reflecting the heavy surface of your anger,
but not what's under it.

Now you're gazing inward like that crazy ape—
dead baby dangling, clutched to her breast
as she scampers over the road.

You swell with a frightful warning:
Get out of here, get away.

You set your face like a table,
your make-up pouch a grenade.

The sun fails. From the still valley of pines
the hum of cicadas rises and vibrates the world.

You listen, those delicate lids three-quarters down:
there are serpents guarding your eyes.

Please talk, I tell you. *I'm frightened, I'm afraid.*
You're a whirlwind threatening terrible excess.

All right, I won't speak till you're ready!
Don't lock yourself in your room.

But I feel the pole in my chest—the oar you've taken up
as you step, with your son, into a small boat.

We were so close! Now you're pushing me, pushing me away—
and rowing out to your island.

A VIEW OF THE SNOWS

This morning I sit to write at my table,
golden oak shipped from America,

and gaze out the window—Himalayan snows
eighty miles off beaming like crystal,

glaciers blazing in distant sunlight
beyond these local hills.

You can walk for hours in view of the snows
on roads carved into slopes: on one side

tree-roots spring from earth above you
while, on the other, you see the topmost branches.

Only two main roads have names in this city:
the Mall Road (for people), the Cart Road (for cars),

so to find any place you have to know it already
or else stop time and again to ask where it is.

But no matter where I walk or what I do,
I never lose the sense of snows around me—

their quiet exalted presence rings my mind,
the shape of who I am flows out to meet them,

a council of jagged elders turned within
so deeply they never feel their mantle of ice.

And even when I cannot see the snows,
when darkness, haze, or rains conceal them,

still I feel their rapt example,
a tiny vision lit in a cave in my heart:

for there is a dimension where such things are true,
and living among them has let me see it

just as I'd come to know a different truth,
or the same truth in a different way,

if I spent my days looking out at a banked volcano.
And I never tire of their lessons. How can I?

The whole intent of the ultimate one,
the one that—if anything can—will save you,

is that it never ends.

ANNIVERSARY

We stayed married too long.
Now this lovely baby beams like an elf
in his nest of toys,

fruit of confusion
who lives in perfect sounds.

What happens next? Drifting in mist,
we pull in all directions at once,

away from that airy gallery
with its brooding models of the true and good.

Look—you are running one night
up those steep hundred steps to the temple
where Mother Kali lives,

and four drunk boys, smirking like cinema hoods,
nudge and abuse you.

You have a crazy temper and you fight
so they do, and soon
their pooled cowardice inflames them

till you lie in front of the temple
smashed like a stone dog.

They leave you now
to the deep enchantment crashing down,

silence a part of the darkness,
the temple monkeys drowned in sleep.

Tell me. What is really important?
What is the last thing you think of?

LATE NOTES

It snowed in the mountains last night!

Now the ice-ranges blaze into life—
fluorescent, white,

a ridge of cracked teeth,

a long soul floating
out of its body.

This is really the end. Soon
I descend to the plains—

that flat heat,
the fountains
spitting out pearls.

Yesterday's letter
spoke of "the parting of ways."

When is this not happening?
The ice-floes erupting in the river—

cracking, heaving
into new alliances.

It is everywhere: sorrow,
restraint, and gentleness.

Are these virtues interchangeable,
a kind of madness?

I wish I had kept a journal of this.
Then all the lies could outlive me.

FROM THE PLAINS
(Hyderabad, India)

Dear A.,

    It may startle you to think
I don't know to whom I am writing.
But it's so.

Outside my window, the bright heat
slows everything down to a shamble—even that cow
rummaging in the garbage moves like a fish
nudging heavy ripples through the air.

Raspberry, mango—bougainvillea spills
in sherbet colors, over the white wall.
And the grinding whine of hawkers' cries
piercing my head. *Vegetables! Lemons! Knives!*
Moans tortured from the rack.

It is bearable inside.
Dressed in loose cotton, unhurried,
I wait out the day.

Every two hours I water the river-grass shades—
their scent visits the air like a ghost of coolness.

Imagine the immense relief of sunset:
this blinding sky softened to bruised pastels,
across it moving black specks, birds—
memories that roost in the heart.

From the massed boulders, the ridge of false mountains,
a breeze descends, but it is feeble.
One drop of water on a burning face.

All day those rocks have collected heat.
Are they trying to turn into diamond?
They are reluctant to give up anything,
and are only a little calmed by the hand of the wind.

The night sky, foggy. Only a few stars shine.

Then the moon mounts the horizon,
huge and molten—a volcano-hole.

No sign of rain. My breathing thickened by dust.

Do you hear, through this, my usual voice—
fast, urgent, stumbling on itself?

Why do I write such a letter,
as if I had a "correspondence," and lived in a story?

I thought I would spare you for once,
and tell you what I pretend you want to know.

Or shall I write of the usual things?
My indecisions, my weird dreams,

the fear that being in love
is over once and for good?

Or something new:
how, in the past year,
as I start my way down the hill,

I loved myself, through you, then lost it.
Through you, and other friends.
Does this make you an agent of *maya*?

You still live in the mountains. How I long to be there!
But I've come to a troubled city
that in all its chaos has no mirrors.

Last month an old friend told me
The stars have gone out of your eyes.
So I am in mourning. Does that make you smile;
did you know, and wonder when I'd come to see it?

I did not know I could be like this—
undone by contingence. I want it not to be so,

but I think of no alternative to the truth.
The problem is, if I turn my back on it,
the stars may go out in the sky.

OUR ELEPHANT

*Last night our elephant remembered India again, in frenzy
he was rending the veil of night till dawn.*
                                        —Jalalluddin Rumi

i.
What if you acclaim
all the images in your poems as visions,
like Blake did?

Visions—you *saw* them

                    wounds
                    that are roses

                    flavors
                    that are tongues

it is all you can do to keep yourself melting to join them,
diving, leaving that self
a dropped robe on the shore.

ii.
The clothing of people in this barren place
exploits a narrow band of color—and their faces

skins

        where are the wild

saffron magenta turquoise purple
black containing all the shades of the rainbow
cruelty embracing every shade of love

a leper's shiny fingerless arm-knobs
smooth as the stumps of an antique chair

life without walls

a barber shaving a man by the side of the road
seated on a rock
before a cracked bit of mirror.

In the searing midday sun
the corpse of an old man, dried piece of pickle,
lies in the street till evening
as you walk back from the market.

iii.
Snows of the Himalayas overlook
the foothills miles away,

December sunshine warming the slopes
where everyone lives outdoors all day in winter.

iv.
The seller of hardboiled eggs
sits in the arc of a cliff
on top of which shines a pink temple

where monkeys lord it over devotees

the egg dipped in a salt/pepper mix
given in a twist of used copybook paper

nothing is wasted here—
there are even shops that refill
those disposable lighters and pens.

v.
From the rooftop watching
Delhi on fire

awakened that night by neighbors:
the water is poisoned!

charred cars, some with bodies still in them

black crusts of buses
shops still smouldering.

A new kind of innocence, this fear
beyond appeal, the object inaccessible—

should a mob swarm to this cut-off house

there is no way to call for help
and nothing,
nothing to be done

vi.
That gentle swami whispers
                          When I close my eyes,
I see so many people crowding around me for blessings.
When I open my eyes, everything is blue.

And the lovely old woman saint: *I see*
your faces lit up by torchlight,
whenever you think of me.

What if it sleeps in your blood, a malarial fever
what if your mind keeps on reliving

what if you never stop remembering
how it felt to live

                    where the destination becomes the path,
                    the flavors become the tongues

ANOTHER ENDING

Your mother came to meet me in a dream—

strong, serene, in potent middle-age,
her silver sari reflecting light,

diamond nose-pin
entrancing the baby.

Somehow you had not known she was still alive,
though for twenty years you had mourned her.

And there was no longer need to pity your father
losing himself in committees and boards of trustees.

Our lives softened and opened.

She tamed the world,
our days would be gracious and sane.

I fell speechless and shy before her,
yet all was accomplished.

Not that the wound had healed:
it had never happened.

You were kind, our marriage unscarred.

I watched you, watching her play
with our son.

This time, I fell in love with the other woman.
The moon moved close,

I was free,
safe
and exalted.

AFTER THE SNOWFALL

AFTER THE SNOWFALL

Months of silence, then a parting of mist.
I heard you say:
It was all your misunderstanding.
My stopped touches
were merely the chill of the wind.

My secretly loving another
had nothing to do with your being lost in the forest,
frozen by my absences.

Those cold letters that choked your breath
were a coffin of snow, growing all night
as you lay there helplessly,
scarred by shadows.

You did not feel
a subsiding of love, but the passionate storm
fitfully dying.

I lied about nothing.
Can't everything be true?
It is not that I do not want you,

but just
that I do not want you.

LOVING SOMEONE ELSE

When it first leaps into being

don't tell me it doesn't shine like a new cloth

so tempting you have to keep opening the closet
to look, to make sure it's there, and it's yours.

While I was dazed in New York
you were here, in the rains, growing.

RE-ENTRY

for Alicia Ostriker

i.
Dear Friend,
            Last June in Muktinath, Nepal,
I climbed too fast to thirteen thousand feet,

got mountain sickness:
headache, violent restlessness, a night
of brightly broken dreams.

I wrote one on the card I sent to you:
You were wearing stilts,
towering above a crowd of women.

"What are your plans?" I asked. You said
"From now on I'm spending a lot of time with my mother."

Three months later, my first night back,
I'm flipping the TV dial in a HoJo motel
and there you are, looking straight into the camera:

...and one of them had a knife. He kept saying
'I don't want to hurt you, I just want money.'
I kept saying, 'I don't want to die,'
and then he raped me.

You looked so strong and sudden!
A quiet child
who finds herself leading an army.

Those stilts—were they crutches?
Or were they simply stilts, were you
uplifted, not broken?

Maybe the stilts were both,

maybe they meant you can be
uplifted by a blow, by what seems
even more irreversible
than everything already is.

ii.
A few days later, another dream assails me:

my fiancé watches—smiling and remote
(as if it were a cute experiment)—

as a man with a knife
slowly cuts off my ears.

After the mutilation I try to act normal, conversing
casually, arranging my hair
to cover the ear-stubs' bloody gristle,
long hair patched with clot.

Then I turn to my lover:
"Seeing how you've behaved,
I don't think I want you any more," but he,

with the money he has stolen from my purse,
is already in a phone booth,
dialing another woman.

A whole, unwounded woman.
                                        I forget her name,
which may be the key to all this, or simply
just another lock.
                        And he is *nothing*—so bland,
one of the least compelling persons
encountered on any journey,
dream or elsewhere: anonymous to the core.

Yet his desertion
hacked another part off the freak I now was—

         "You're so lovely,"
         he'd said once.

iii.
Following this implied confusion in the ranks

I notice things appearing to collapse
into a shimmering lake—the size of this O —

a jewel, an orifice, mouth of a waking dream,
and the dream is limitless.
                                        But you bring along

lunch and a sweater, because it takes
such a long time to get nowhere.

YOU MADE ME LOVE YOU

When the key turned,
the lock fainted.

My arm
behind my back

cracked and I said
"This

is what I always wanted."
Then

on one knee,
my loosed arm bobbing

in its tub of pain,
I looked up

and saw
in a mirror

the nature of blame.
Who

had jumped out
to live there? No one

but me. No one
no one

but me: I ask you
to rule my life,

and this is what
I make of it.

IMPOSSIBLE CHOICES

I have gotten involved again in an erotic relationship with her. I have told her that my first choice is to have a genuine reconciliation with you, but if you do not want that, then she can leave her husband and move in with me. If she doesn't have that choice she will go along with her husband.

Do you believe in slow motion?

There's an orange-scented breeze here
in front of the firing squad,
and perhaps I honor convention in finding
everything sparkling and clear

as if, after harrowing illness, I see

the mossy wall behind me, emerald green,
the perfect mouths of the rifle-barrels,
those shapely trigger fingers,

as marvels known for the first time.

I must have thought it would last forever,
that soothing fetal driftingness

but emotions refuse to keep pace with events—
I scream "I hate you," sick with a fear
that never again will I love like this,

yet the script is exigent—not only with life of its own,
but it *is* the life into which we slide
as only Cinderella fits the slipper.

A choice, an echo? Or one of those trick pictures
you see as a vase *or* a profile, but not both
at the same time?

You conclude: *Make up your mind.*
You know well enough who I am,

but do I? These last few years
the worst I imagined was never enough,

and this personful of contempt and doubletalk
who tries to pass off as my choice his bastard decision

is light-years away from one I once admired,
but that's not the end of the world: it's only me
in respect to whom you've become so degraded

and only you who will ever cause me
to erupt into one of those furies of hell,

remember them? And you know what else?
I have never looked better than now,
I swear it—utterly ravishing
in front of the firing squad,
because it's not really the end, is it?—
I seem to have plenty of time to consider your words,
the slow cortège of bullets swimming through air,

time to view each as well as the whole,
and say:

Now *wait* a minute....

KALI YUGA

You begin you remember that day,
all day you felt colder and colder
until you wondered if warmth could ever again
ripen and console you.

As the wondering lengthened: is it only *you*
or is it the darkness that seems to be falling
everywhere, gathering daily, weekly—
is it truly out there, the darkness there

falling like snow in urgent silence
(snow falling in the form of darkness: the last snow, only
we don't know it yet, not most of us)
because it will never end?
Will it be the last snow because it will never end?

And meanwhile our lives are hard, our fortunate lives
easy, shut-in and fearful.
Miracles, sources of joy—one's child—
but still it is so hard
because of the darkness, darkness that began
as spaces among flakes of light,
spaces swarming, blotting up sweetness

until, in the final moments, all that remains
is the consolation that at last we deserve a savior,

things so bad we need a savior to come,
or else we won't get saved

                          come help us save
our lives, our illusion of necessity.

"WHEN EVERYTHING YOU DO IS A MIRROR"

That day I suddenly saw you
across an acre of lawn at the posh hotel

I would not raise my eyes

I held my white teacup and talked to a man
who said something about New York,
his trip in the fifties,

and stared at me boldly—a foreign woman
with unbound hair—but I barely heard him,

floating outside of myself to the edge of the lawn

where pink bougainvillea blew in the March wind,
hundreds of butterflies pinned to the bushes

I would not meet your gaze

though I knew you were trying to lever my eyes
and sideways I saw you swallow a smile

conceding this round to me, as one among many—
a pretty pass of the cape, but there would be others

you never thought this could be the last time
you would ever see me.

PRONOUNS

i.
So you've lost him. Or you've lost it.

And night after night after year
the dreams wash over you, leaching your
vitality,
          waves
building a lining enriched
thickened
expelled: you

don't need them, any more
than you need a hundred barely-begun
aborted lives

before the real one arrives—one that quickens,
guides you to death, your own
encoded unfurling of sails,
moist wings, membranes
that light you on your way.

Opals. A nursery of shimmering iridescences

green, pink, blue, the tongues disappearing
into nuances of time—

no need for that now.
You want clarity. It wants you,

wants explanations of your life,
of what gets born before

attainment and loss:
those come later, not as afterthought

but afterbirth, your own particular
nightmares repeating
what you don't want to hear.

ii.
A recurring nightmare of photographs
in the home you've discovered at last:

part houseboat, part cottage, part villa,
set in the mountains yet near the sea,

sunlight supporting you, warming the benches,
cascades of flowers in your garden;
the cleansing air of the beaches
entering your flung-wide windows.

Your ideal physical home, except
for the photographs you never knew were there
until you had moved in forever.

The photographed past stashed everywhere,
generous closets infested

with photographs of you,
of him, of her,
of them, of you then,
of you further back then,

of your childhood, your marriage,
the one you spent twenty-five years with,

till the glimpse of a photograph's edge makes you wince,
the merest bit a hologram containing
all that it is, in every dimension.

Photographs strewn on the Persian carpets,
over the sill of an open doorway,

lining the mantelpiece, even impaled
on the shining brass of the poker:

everywhere, everywhere, even when unseen,
the unpainted sun the source of light in a painting,

so you
know you can never feel settled,

never again
begin again
until all those images get sorted and labelled,
images of you and in you expelled,

thousands of images laid to rest in their albums
in an order you have chosen

the task seeming endless, appalling, the task
that will go on taking forever
until you are ready to begin.

DIVORCE, ETC.

There is a house
at the end of a street—

spacious   calm   light

with a deep porch all around,
and a heart that is sound.

Stories gather on the sills at evening,
friendly adventures ending in home.

Lamps ripen in impending dusk,
candle-flames of souls in chorus,
a single note piercing every one—

the fireplace sang,
wind moved in our branches
as in summer, which trades daylight
for the glow of innerness,
candle-glow of bodiless souls
(a single note ignites them, rumor
drenching the crowd).

The house had everything.
On one side, wooded—a solitude
wounded by absence. And healed.

One side facing neighbors,
a peaceful street

like the flesh of a pregnant woman
whose symphony of cells
spins love from her body
(a single fate unites them),

a chain electrocution,
the family herded off
by the killer:

they know he will kill them,
know what they might do,
yet are never quite ready to act.

And upstairs, near the window
where sunlight gilds a child's collection of shells—

perfection of spirals,
elated forms!—
whoever wonders what their lives were like,
the lives of these creatures that lived
inside such beauty?

HOW IT IS NOW

All night long I kept trying to reach you
but obstacles bloomed like magic towers

and even at noon, the road where you live
lay hushed in impenetrable shadows.

No matter how quickly I ran to you in my mind,
your house remained always around the bend

so I could not even see you at work in your garden
or glimpse the sunset flash in the glass of your door.

All this time I was trapped in another dimension
back at the palace, a famous hotel

gone to seed in its fabulous setting—
acres of lawn looking out on unmelting snows.

I wanted to leave, but somehow was forced
to try out for a play, though the script was bizarre

and I'd never acted: a man and a woman
live out their lives in bed.

Then the audition ended, but now
my mother appeared, demanding to drive me

wherever it was I was going. I knew
if she came along I would never arrive.

At last I rushed off—would you still be there?
It was nearly dark as I rounded the bend

and found that my little boy was walking beside me,
holding my hand. I would have to go all the way back.

I knew then that there would always be something else,
I would never reach you again, and maybe

the dreadful ending must be this way:
I had made my choices, and this was where they had led me—

to a place from which I look back and see
your godly devotion shrunk to a dog in the road,

and you beyond anything I do or say.
Yet still, like a madwoman finding her cage unlocked,

my shadow leaps naked and frenzied, out
in the silent night—and turns and runs

towards innocent pastures where every dream,
even this dream of you,

slips free of its meanings.

THE DREAM OF ELIZABETH HARTLEY

i.
Here on the prison lawn, a veil
of sunlight weights the grass.

I walk here, while my brother
is visiting the warden who is his friend.

I am never to understand why my brother
wants to bring his troupe of actors,

the mesmerist who leads them into
the lives of fictions, and leaves them there.

Years later, he is long since blind;
I ask him, but he cannot remember

this day's excursion, or that I have been the companion
who waits, in the sullen heat, on these deep green lawns.

ii.
The narrow windows of the reading room,
through a trick of light,

are blind eyes reflecting the sky.
I cross to them, my long skirts trailing the grass,

and enter the cool room.
It is grave as a church—

books, simple chairs,
a long table

from which, unthinking, I pick up a sheaf of pages
and start to read.

It is a poem
that pulls me instantly into its steady music.

A key turns in a lock
I never knew was there.

iii.
What could it mean to be a man
stripped of freedom, writing like this?

And then he is beside me,
the author of this poem.

Tall, lean, a shadowed face—
his name is Rawley

and somehow I know his life
as if it were a past life of my own.

I know that he killed a comrade,
but not with a gun.

Failed love was the weapon;
the man, his twin.

It was somehow himself that he killed,
he was the victim.

iv.
Our talk unwinds
as light drains from the room.

I have fallen
into a way of speech I never suspected,

years of the closest knowing
compressed in these two small hours.

Face to face,
no veils between us—

I am seeing myself in a mirror
where there is no mirror.

My mind no longer whispers
what I am doing.

v.
We speak of everything! We speak of the soul.
As a child, I tell him, I often thought

if my soul is immortal it must be very old,
it must reach back,

it must have housed itself
in someone else, before it entered me.

And somewhere,it seems,in this endless chain of unhousings
we must have been fiercely wed.

We have walked by an opal lake,
the far shore shimmering pastel,

and above it, one white peak
rising up like the ghost from a deathbed.

Beneath its shadow, an undreamt kingdom—
hues full and clear as bells,

the blues and reds of violets, roses.
It is so quiet, even the silence has ended.

vi.
After this day we do not meet again,
or write one single line.

How is there need
for further words of comfort or of love?

And as I turn away, I see
my future as the portrait of my past.

How I shall never marry—my husband is here—
but lead my brother into his failing sight.

Day after day, waking from dreams
whose story is lost, though the grieving pursues me.

My life a reproach and a torment—
an ugly woman with a beautiful name.

vii.
Long years from now, the hour of his death,
I receive the news that Rawley has died,

and the page on which he wrote his epitaph.
These words are carved on his tombstone!

>   *May God In Heaven Save My Soul*
>   *For You, Elizabeth Hartley*

And the pain of this separation is not worse
than the years before, that shadow

staining each step I took without him,
the smiles of the children I never bore.

At least he was free,
knowing he had no choices.

viii.
I imagine the release of his soul—
a speck of foam falling back to a heaving ocean,

waves arched like trees, or the necks of horses.
And now he is everywhere, nowhere:

an exaltation,
an indelible wound.

ix.
My brother spoke of a saint—limbs all hacked off,
who in extremity cried out to God, *More pain!*

How can I comprehend this? Yet now,
like a far-off torch borne through a sleeping forest,

the light stabs out to me. Is it a gift?
Is grace the name of such pain?—

the more you receive,
the more you are driven within,

and when pain is only a cloak,
a disguise of the body,

you are thrust—through the needle's eye—
to where oneness is?

x.
Rawley, I had a dream. I was riding alone
in an open carriage, deep into alien country.

There were grasses, trees—yet the fields
blew empty of life.

No signs of life, except
for two blind stallions plunging like waves before me.

I stopped, climbed down to the road.
I never heard sounds so clear—

the horses' wheezing, the whish of their tails.
The exhausted sighings of wood and leather.

Weight after weight
lifted from me like veils,

all pain dissolved
in the spasm of being what is!

xi.
I see you locked bodiless in space—
unable to see or speak, yet everywhere

sound and vision,
while I

am trapped inside my body,
the red locked into its rose.

Can it be there is nothing you feel,
yet nothing you do not know?

Outside my room, the sky
spills black and huge into fields

carved open like bellies, wet for sowing.
I have lived out my life like a ghost at a party!

You know what I want to say:
We are both in prison.

THAT CHILD

WINTER BIRTH

Why should I wake at four in the morning
into my mind, already up and singing
I am thirty-seven, I have a new baby,
how can I live with a man I no longer trust?

My breasts aching, flushed with milk—
but the baby sleeps.

When he sucks, he looks up at me
wide-eyed, adoring,

the eyes of a deer in the first garden
before he learns
man can't be trusted.

I want to walk where my head is light,
on a path lit only by stars,
in the still and compassionate mountains.

I want to say to the god inside

Only pick me up and hold me,
I too will stop crying.

VENTRILOQUIST

I speak in words so you will understand

I am strong as you need,
large as whatever you want.

You already know this,
but you are afraid.

You have witnessed miracles,
yet you fear that word.

A lightning pierced you, flashing you on and on,

petals in flickering rings
surrounding the heart in its tower!

Your mind talked wildly but it did not matter,
locked in the currents of that blazing flower.

You sit and hope that it will come again—
knowing it happens once, and you go on

to something new you could not imagine,
a new birth of the death of innocence.

But what could you love better than this loss,

running in circles, trying to feign
the sweetness of wanting nothing?

And if nothing comes, that too is a lesson—
only its coming is longer and harder.

> Work. Write.
> Look after the child.
> Your freedoms chained in light.

OLD LIGHT

"Mom," my nine-year-old says,
*"you know this light might be from
when the dinosaurs were alive.
Some light is really old light."*

Long ago light spilling into
a future so distant, the past
can never again happen
in just the same way:

where a woman like me,
child grown and gone,
looks back at herself, prehistoric—

slowly in the mountains of Nepal
trekking up Muktinath
to thirteen thousand feet,

first through a riverbed gorge,
its stones
marked like charms,
most with white ovals

hours and hours moving upward,
alone: nothing happens,
though anything could

out there

where you've entered the frontier
so whoever you are
could not possibly matter

while you've been so busy
holding a stone
stamped with a snowy mountain:

the rest of living
could have been like this—
wings, not anchors
out on the edge

out on the edge, back
in the good old light

THAT CHILD

*...knowledge of ourselves and others and of the
surroundings implies knowledge of distinction and
difference...*
                    S. Shankaranarayanan, *Sri Chakra*

When the baby
enters the world

affirming two
where there was one, departing

the world of a mother's body,
setting out for the horizon of
its human fate—

the world a view
from a wide wide window,
long before objects have names;

then the baby gazes, doesn't yet name what is,
doesn't need to know names, poised as he is to begin
that long dependent childhood

exuding the drug-bond of need,
his need and yours:

the power to create and fulfill need,
induce and relieve it.

I wish I could have another baby.
I've got
my nine-year-old son,
divine addiction,

but that's just it: and there's conflict already,
his sturdy selfhood already a mask,
a stone's throw
from the stony otherness of manhood.

Slowly withdrawing his need, he creates and abandons
the slashed flesh of our life;
and what should those edges heal up with?

He's off for a summer with his father.
So I smile and work,
yet hang suspended:
my outline a field of dots
appearing solid
only from far away.

There's a footpath in the hills up here
in the lower Himalayas,
a small path in the mountains of India.

Moonless night
where lights alongside the road have failed,
and the sky is bright with stars.

Midnight, and I'm walking on this road
completely alone,
fearless—there's not much to fear.

The beam of my flashlight probes, exposes
pebbles with the gravity of mountains,
moths—they're feathery jewels—
one small brown scorpion corpse.

Round slabs of cowdung
like stepping-stones dropped
to mark your way out of the forest.

You truly can see the Milky Way—
intimate, nearly touchable,
stars splashed over a sky

glued to the ceiling of the room so deeply imagined
for the child it's too late to have,
to help her feel safe in the dark—

millions, millions of stars overlooking
this path of the life I've chosen.

AFTERWORD

The poems in this collection have been shaped by India. Beginning in 1969, I made many short visits; and I lived there for an extended period, from 1975-85. Much of the time I spent in Simla, in the foothills of the Himalayas. When the weather is clear, you can see, in several directions, snowpeaks more than twenty thousand feet high. For me, this kept things in perspective; or created a perspective on which I grew to depend.

Sometimes I visited ashrams and sat with spiritual teachers. And I practiced the discipline of meditation. But living in India, accepting as commonplace what here it seems commonplace to reject; accepting frustrations and inconveniences—that is also a discipline. Things you think you can't do without, that you considered virtual necessities, you manage without—and even though you would rather have them, it is refreshing to experience how these notions of what you require are a kind of trap. And it never really gets resolved; or for me it hasn't. In India, I do without (water taps, electricity, toilets, or telephones that work; cars with seatbelts; safe roads; access to good hospitals); then back to America, and after a very short while, the illusion of what is indispensable once again takes hold. And I also grow accus- tomed to not having the spiritual sustenance I take for granted in India; and the much greater variety of people I know, the kind of culture in which the importance of social relations adjusts the pace of life. I can't imagine anyone there saying, "I'm very busy—but let's have lunch in a couple of weeks."

In 1975, I began a long, intermittently-pursued project of translating, with help from various writers and scholars, some wonderful 12th-century South Indian bhakti poems composed by mystics who spoke Kannada, which is still the language of present-day Karnataka. The manuscript centers on the work of the woman "saint-poet" Mahadeviyakka. Her lyrics, and those of others in her group, *must* have influenced me deeply because I love what they say, and how they say it. No mystical poems I have ever read have been so consistently accessible, direct, and moving. Just how this "influence" appears—that I can't quite say. But if this writing has mattered so much to my life, it has in some way entered my work.

One other note. About twenty years ago, I was working on my Ph.D. dissertation on Sylvia Plath. What impressed me most about the language and quality of mind evident in her best poems was how completely I could trust her. On level after level, she seems to be in control of meaning—even in poems which seem fueled by almost uncontrollable emotion. Look up a key word or reference—ariel or purdah, ivory, jade, stasis—and intricate underlying harmonies are revealed. For me, this being responsible for every word is an ideal, even if I usually forget about it, even though it doesn't mean I can do it myself. And the more I trusted Plath, the more I trusted that she never used words or references superficially. So when she mentioned Zen in a published poem, and in some of her drafts, of course I had to read something about Zen Buddhism, so I'd know what she was talking about. Before I knew it, I had virtually stopped work on my thesis, and for more than a year I read spiritual texts. One thing leads to another, and I follow (this is how I feel my poetry goes).

Study, exploration, are very important to me. After returning to America I studied Sanskrit for several years, though for no formal reason. Also, informally, I have studied ayurveda, an ancient Indian system of medicine. If I had unlimited years to live, I would probably spend most of them in study. Discovery has been a great pleasure. As has been raising a child of two cultures, constantly changing, and learning what I'm like as a mother. It's this same curiosity—to find out what's going to happen, what's about to happen, what's supposed to happen, that pulls me through a poem, almost like in the mystery novels I keep reading. And that's how my writing has been for at least fifteen years now. All of this shapes my poetry, and also adds to the distractions that keep me from writing.

The last two lines of "Our Elephant" are adapted from "The Secret of Natural Devotion" in Jananadeva's "Amritanubhava," translated by B.P. Bahirat. The quotation from Rumi is from A.J. Arberry's translation, "Mystical Poems of Rumi." "When Everything You Do Is a Mirror" is a phrase borrowed from Steve Orlen. The first line of "Thinking about History" is attributed to R. Buckminster Fuller

It was a Thursday when I lifted the phone and called my agent. I said, "Gabe, I'm going to be sixty-six tomorrow, Friday, January 13, 1978, and I've been writing fiction all my life and no one's ever published a word of it and I'd give my left pinkie to get into *The Paris Review*." And I did because Gabriel was interested at once and told me that he'd get in touch with me the next day because he thought he might find a buyer. He did. . . . When my story came out, I went to Dr. Dodypol and had the finger removed surgically and under anesthesia. His head nurse, Kate Crackernuts, wrapped the finger in cotton bandages and in red tissue paper with a yellow ribbon around it and I walked out a published author and weighing three ounces less than when I walked in.

—*Dallas Wiebe, "Night Flight to Stockholm," Issue 73*

THE PARIS REVIEW

"A Prestigious Launching Pad for Young Writers."

—The Boston Globe